Birds of New Zealand

A Nature Travel Guide

If you do not speak, you can hear nature speaking around you; If you move quietly and stop smoothly, nature will see you as less of a threat; Before walking into the open, wait at the edge and look around; Love nature, be loved in return.

My name is Duncan and I am the author of this travel guide. Clearly the vastness of the internet exists. However, I still believe this book is useful: It offers unbiased comparisons of a carefully chosen selection of places seen through the same pair of eyes; It describes what you might realistically see; It includes clear directions to make your trip run more smoothly.

My email is drduncanjames@gmail.com and I welcome your feedback and questions. A positive review really helps and if this travel guide doesn't work for you perhaps tell me so that I can try to fix it both for you and for other readers.

Perhaps the best starting point when reading this book is the New Zealand chapter as this is an overview of the whole country and includes summaries of most of the other chapters.

Location and site numbering refers to the numbers on the maps.

A capitalised animal name refers to a single species; A non-capitalised animal name refers to a group of animals of more than one species.

Barn Owl 5x2 (m3) means Barn Owl was seen 5 times, the average group size was 2 and the maximum seen in one group was 3.

You might also like to get an "identification guide" or "field guide" to help identify the animals you see.

The maps are for general guidance only. The GPS coordinates are generally accurate to 5 metres.

The most dangerous animals on planet Earth are the humans. It is recommended that you use travel safety resources http://www.gov.uk/foreign-travel-advice to stay safe. Other predators include bears and crocodiles. Animals with powerful defences such as snakes and wasps can also be a danger. Finally, the environment around you can have hazards such as fast tides, deep mud and remote paths.

This is part of the Nature Travel Guide series. Other books in the series cover different countries and one covers general wildlife watching skills.

The chapter numbering corresponds to the numbers on the maps; so it is not sequential.

Table of Contents

New Zealand (Australasia)

"Unique island wildlife that includes the difficult to see, nocturnal kiwis."

My favourite location is **Stewart Island** which has avoided some of the damage from non-native, invasive wildlife.

New Zealand is a group of islands in the Pacific Ocean, just east of Australia. For many, the main reason to visit New Zealand for wildlife are the kiwi https://www.kiwisforkiwi.org and the other unique flightless birds found nowhere else in the world. However, New Zealand wildlife evolved without many natural predators: the damage done by introduced, non-native predators such as rat, possum, Stoat and Ferret has been massive.

Other countries with damaged ecosystems (which is most countries) have more natural predators, so the native species have more evasion and defence skills. My personal experience is that the wildlife of New Zealand feels very limited away from the protected reserves. However, I still enjoyed seeing the unique native wildlife at the protected reserves and islands.

The main three islands are North Island, South Island and Stewart Island. North Island and South Island have slightly different animal and plant species so, for example, birdwatchers typically visit both.

Stewart Island generally has the same species as South Island. However, Stewart Island is smaller so it has been slightly easier to control non-native predators. It also has less non-native plants which can make the experience feel closer to how it would have been before humans colonised.

There are all the usual types of accommodation in New Zealand. If you are on a budget and sufficiently hardy then "freedom camping" enables you to camp for free away from regulated areas (typically this prohibits camping in more popular tourist areas, in some national parks and within 500m of commercial campsites). Transport can be difficult as this is a country where many depend on a car. I used public coaches and still saw a lot of wildlife. You might choose to hire a car or, if on a longer trip, buy an old car to resell when you leave.

Location Summaries

Locations in bold each have their own chapter later in the book.

There are also summaries of other chapters about New Zealand at the end of the list.

Kahurangi (location 1) is an extensive forest with surviving, native wildlife that includes giant snails, giant worms, Great Spotted Kiwi and other birds. Coastal wildlife can be seen at Golden Bay.

Paparoa (location 2) is another extensive forest with native wildlife including Great Spotted Kiwi and other birds. The coastline at Punakaiki includes a White-fronted Tern colony and a Westland Petrel colony.

Haast (location 3) has coastline and forest with Fiordland Crested Penguin and Yellowhead in small numbers.

Fiordland (location 4) has scenic views that are popular with tourists. Native birds including Yellowhead can be seen in the fern-rich forests and dolphins can be seen on the sounds.

Stewart Island (location 5) has escaped some of the introduced plants and predators of the main islands. The native plantlife is therefore slightly more intact. The small size of the island and keen, local volunteers has also made it possible to develop predator-free areas with healthy populations of native birds.

The **South East Coast (location 6)** has seabirds all year round, particularly in summer. There are cliffs with nesting albatrosses, shags and gulls. Many beaches have burrows just inland with nesting penguins.

The mountains around **Mount Cook (location 7)** have specialist alpine plants. Nearby are braided rivers with the rare Black Stilt and Wrybill.

Franz Josef (location 8) is on the western side of Mount Cook which is the more popular side for hikers to start on. Walks here have views of the mountains, native forest and native birds. The Okarito Brown Kiwi and Great Egret are found slightly to the north, near the coast.

Kaikoura (location 9) is a top whale-watching and dolphin-watching destination because the continental shelf is near to the shore. Strong water currents form at the continental shelf (which is a steep depth-change between the coast and deep sea). These currents flush nutrients into the water, encouraging plankton and other small animals which are then eaten by fish, birds, dolphins and whales. I have only briefly visited but many others have reported their sightings and scientific surveys provide population data. Adolescent male Sperm Whales are resident (who apparently can have scars from fighting giant squid). Humpback Whales migrate past in June/July. Orca are seen from December to February. The Kaikoura Mountains hold the early 21st century's only known breeding site https://en.wikipedia.org/wiki/Kowhai_Valley_and_Shearwater_Stream_Important_Bird_Area for Hutton's Shearwater. For a morning or evening view as they fly overhead, follow Mount Fyffe Road north from Kaikoura to Fyffe Palmer Bush Walk and the Kowhai Valley. At Mount Fyffe Hut (a basic hiking hut) Hutton's Shearwater can be heard flying overhead at night. Relocations http://www.huttonsshearwater.org.nz/ are developing new colonies, including one near the town. The Peninsula Walkway leads south from town with views of fur seals. You can see Red-billed Gull and Black-billed Gull scavenge around the benches while Kelp Gull and Pied Shag fly offshore.

The Marlborough Sounds (location 10) is a large collection of islands, bays and cliffs on the north of South Island. Motuara Island surveys report South Island Saddleback, South Island Robin and other native forest birds. Blumine Island surveys report Orange-fronted Parakeet and other native birds. Water taxis can take you to these island nature reserves. Kaipupu Point is a reserve just north of Picton protected by a predator fence with access by water taxi. A popular tramping/hiking route called Queen Charlotte Track goes from Anakiwa along some beautiful coast to Ship Cove.

The ferry between Picton and Wellington across the **Cook Strait (location 11)** offers the chance to watch the sea for wildlife.

Wellington (location 12) has nearby nature reserves Kapiti Island and Zealandia which are protected from non-native predators and have growing populations of native birds and other wildlife.

Hastings (location 13) is on the southern end of Hawke's Bay, on the east coast of North Island. As with all the coast of New Zealand, others report that it is good for wildlife watching. Hastings is particularly well known for the Australasian Gannet colony at Cape Kidnappers. Ahuriti Estuary at Napier is mentioned by others as good for birds. Boundary Stream nature reserve to the north is a popular destination for birdwatchers.

Auckland (location 14) has a number of sites that are within one or two hour's drive. Wading birds such as New Zealand Dotterel, a colony of Australasian Gannets and other wildlife can be seen.

The Department of Conservation (DoC) runs a Black Stilt centre http://www.doc.govt.nz/parks-and-recreation/places-to-go/canterbury/ places/twizel-area/kaki-black-stilt-visitor-hide/ near Twizel. In general, the Braided Rivers (location 15) on the east side of the central mountains are known for Black Stilt, Wrybill and other wetland birds. The DoC ask visitors to not stray from trails. Others have seen Black Stilt and New Zealand Scaup in the wetland areas just west of Twizel. Other braided rivers are the Rangitata River and Rakaia River above Methven, although they are difficult explore if you are reliant on public transport. O Tu Wharekai http://www.doc.govt.nz/otuwharekai is a top wetland nature reserve in this area. Others also visit Ashburton Lakes http://www.christchurchnz.com/walk-canterbury/mid-canterbury/ashburt on-lakes-and-hakatere-park/ for wetland wildlife. (GPS coords 44.2648S 170.1031E)

Arthur's Pass (location 16) has easy public transport access (for example, from Greymouth). The easiest-reached parts (within a day's walk of Arthur's Pass) are not generally considered to be so good for birdwatching. The Hawdon valley is home to the endangered Orange-fronted Parakeet. Otira Gorge is known as a good place to see Rock Wren and Blue Duck.

Rivers flow from the volcanoes in the centre of North Island to feed the many large forests such as Pureora http://www.thetimbertrail.com/ Forest Park, **Whirinaki (location 17)** and Te Urewera. Pureora is often visited as a day trip by birdwatchers, partly because it is easy to access from Auckland. Large parts of Te Urewera are privately owned making access more difficult. I chose Whirinaki to explore because of its scenic, ancient forest.

Cape Foulwind (location 18) is home to a seal colony 10km west of Westport that is easy to add to a driving itinerary and is visited by many of the organised coach tours.

Birdwatching in New Zealand varies between protected and non-protected areas and the different islands which have different native species.

I recommend a number of birdwatching itineraries for New Zealand from short visits of a few days to longer, budget backpacking trips of a few weeks.

Additional Location Possibilities

There is a lot of crossover between these wildlife-watching locations and generally-popular, outdoor destinations. Other popular places to enjoy outdoor pursuits include the Whanganui River where you can do a multi-day canoe/kayak trip with wild camping and also Tongariro. Maps for all of New Zealand http://www.topomap.co.nz are available online.

Banded Plover can be seen on beaches all around the coast of New Zealand.

Wildlife of New Zealand

I often recommend a bird identification guide; In the case of New Zealand I think the bird species are distinctive enough that almost any of the available guides will work well. I simply recommend checking that a guide includes all the native species and not just the commonly seen ones (and obviously both native and non-native birds if this is important for you). I actually created my own guide to the native species by gluing pictures onto some sheets of paper and adding basic written notes to reduce the weight of my rucksack. Regarding non-native birds, I was happy identifying them from having already seen them in other countries. The bird overview chapter later in this book has some specific identification advice.

The parks and gardens have lots of non-native Blackbird, Song Thrush, House Sparrow, Greenfinch, Goldfinch, Chaffinch, Dunnock, Starling, Australian Magpie and Mallard. Native Paradise Shelduck are common. Other native birds such as Bellbird, Tui, Silvereye and Grey Warbler can also be seen, but in my experience not in the same numbers as the non-natives which seem to be better able to adapt to urban habitats.

Small islands that have been completely cleared of predators and turned into nature reserves include Tiritiri Matangi Island, Kapiti Island and Ulva Island which are open to the public. The experience on these nature reserves (which typically have fewer introduced plants as well) is obviously closer to the pre-human New Zealand experience.

There are also many other nature-reserve islands such as Codfish Island https://en.wikipedia.org/wiki/Codfish_Island and Putauhina Island off Stewart Island, Little Barrier Island http://www.doc.govt.nz/parks-and-recreation/places-to-go/auckland/places/little-barrier-island-nature-reserve-hauturu-o-toi/know-before-you-go/ in the Hauraki Gulf, Stephen's Island between North and South Island that is home to the largest population of Tuatara lizard in the early 21st century and Breaksea Island and Chalky Island in Fiordland that have very limited access to the public. A strong research community http://notornis.osnz.org.nz/ is working to help preserve/save the wildlife of these islands. These less-accessible islands are valuable as "ark populations" of native wildlife.

There are more and more "island" reserves being created and populated on mainland New Zealand. These are protected by fences and include Zealandia near Wellington and Tawharanui Open Sanctuary north of Auckland. Many other areas of the mainland have significant anti-predator measures which are not as good as a fence but still help the native wildlife to recover.

Further offshore are more islands that are also part of New Zealand. The Chatham Islands are relatively large and have a resident population with regular flights, but it is still fairly expensive to visit. Cruises to the tiny, isolated and rocky Subantarctic Islands are popular with more wealthy wildlife-watching tourists.

New Zealand's isolated position means the only native land-based mammal is a bat, with native birds having evolved to fill the environmental niches often taken by mammals elsewhere. This unique native birdlife is part of a unique nature experience. It also means that these birds are very vulnerable to predators because they lay their eggs on the ground.

Introduced species to New Zealand http://www.doc.govt.nz/nature/pests-and-threats/animal-pests/animal-pests-a-z/ include deer, goats, chamois, possums, Stoat, Weasel, Ferret, rats and mice. The deer will eat fresh shoots on trees and bushes meaning the forest can be slow to regrow. Deer have in the past reached pest proportions and hunting now controls their numbers. (It is thought that the now extinct moa may have grazed fresh shoots meaning the impact of deer could be beneficial or at least not as bad as it might seem.) Goats and chamois can potentially have a similar impact to deer. Possums were introduced from Australia where they mainly eat vegetation and do significant damage to the native trees. In New Zealand the introduced possums have become larger than the source population in Australia and (based on scientific monitoring data) a significant part of the possum's diet has become the eggs of birds which is impacting native bird numbers. Rats and mice also eat bird eggs. The Stoat is becoming "public enemy number one" as scientists are learning that this one species has maybe had the largest impact of all on native birds: For example, the crash in population of the Yellowhead in the 2010's is thought to have been primarily caused by the Stoat. However, the "public enemy number one" title is difficult to win and the impact of possums on the forest (by eating the fresh stems of the trees) and the egg-eating habits of the rat put them in the running as well.

Pests are dealt with using hunting, trapping and also poisoning. The poisoning uses a bait in the form of pellets that are dropped from the sky containing a poison called 1080. This is a natural chemical found in plants. If the bait is not eaten, it disintegrates in rain and becomes part of the natural background concentration of this chemical that is found everywhere. To minimise impact on other wildlife the bait is designed to appeal specifically to the target predators which includes giving it a slight taste of cinnamon. 1080 is banned in many other countries due to the danger to mammals: the lack of native mammals has made its use an option in New Zealand.

Species of bird that it is too late to save include the many different species of moa. Moa are a large, flightless bird which was hunted to extinction by the Maori. (I like to talk about the moa in present tense to make the extinction feel more real and also because I like to think we can develop our DNA technology and behavioural-biology knowledge far enough to bring them back from the dead.) Many species of waterbird such as duck and wader (waders are known as shorebirds in American English) have also gone extinct, perhaps because of the ease with which wetland birds can be hunted: However, this does not tell the whole story because many smaller forest birds now have populations that are so small that conservationists are having to work very hard to save them.

Whales, dolphins, seals, sea lions, gannets, albatross, terns, shags, penguins and other wildlife live around the coast of New Zealand. However, some places are better to visit than others because of a combination of: good views from clifftops; protected cliff habitats; small offshore rock stacks that provide safe nest sites; conservation efforts; nutrient uplift from the continental shelf (as at Kaikoura) and; special viewing areas with information boards and other keen visitors that make the wildlife easier to see.

Fur seals share the same overall shape, external ears and ability to walk on their flippers with sea lions. This photograph shows a fur seal. Compared to a sea lion, the fur seal lacks the flaps of blubber (they instead rely on their fur to keep them warm) and the fur seal is also smaller.

Skinks and geckos (both of whom can lose their tails to avoid predators) are the only native lizards in New Zealand with about 80 species living today. Geckos have large heads and skinks are generally more slender with more narrow heads. I have heard of many people seeing skinks, including in urban areas. I personally got 3 or 4 brief views during a 2 month visit to New Zealand.

I enjoyed exploring the remnants of the native forest. The large trees include Southern Beech and Podocarps. These tall trees are very good at taking the light from the sun, meaning very little light reaches the ground. Trying to take photographs on the forest floor can be difficult. I saw lots of epiphytes; these are plants that have evolved to survive without soil, living on the branches of the trees high up where there is still sunlight available. On the ground the slow-growing ferns and tree ferns are able to survive with less light.

Tuatara are mainly nocturnal with some very strong island populations. They are rare on the mainland. Zealandia and Invercargill are two good places to see captive populations that are active during the day.

Flax is an iconic New Zealand plant that is popular with Bellbirds and Silvereye who feed on the nectar of the flowers.

Black marks on many of the trees in New Zealand are Sooty Mould. Insects damage the tree, honeydew is released and the mould grows on the sugars.

Many people want to see a kiwi when they visit New Zealand. This is a Southern Brown Kiwi. I saw it during the day at Mason Bay on Stewart Island. They can be seen during the day at Mason Bay which is a reward for the 3 day hike to get there (or just 1 day if you use the river taxi to get partway). It is a grainy photograph because it was in a dark area under the trees.

Weta are an insect related to crickets that live in the forests of New Zealand. Naturalists report that they are mainly nocturnal, although they can sometimes be seen during the day. I photographed this one in the hut at Mason Bay on Stewart Island.

These wooden boxes are traps. They are often baited with eggs which is a great way of selectively killing predators that are likely to go for the nests of native birds.

Location 1: Kahurangi (New Zealand)

Kahurangi, New Zealand

"Home of the Heaphy Trail and Great Spotted Kiwi."

On my hike here I saw and heard Great Spotted Kiwi at Gouland Downs and in the Forest Below James Mackay Hut.

Kahurangi national park http://www.doc.govt.nz/parks-and-recreation/places-to-go/nelson-tasman/places/kahurangi-national-park/ is a large, wild forest combined with higher ground. The high ground has alpine wildlife including Kea, Rock Wren and Mountain Beech. The bogs have native plants including endemic species of asphodel and foxglove. As with all of New Zealand, there are problems with predators but some predator-control measures are in place.

This location description is based on my visit in spring 2016 when I was attracted by the stable population of Great Spotted Kiwi in the forest. The natural population is so strong that it is even being used for translocations to boost the numbers in other areas.

Site Summaries

The Gouland Downs (site 1) is one of the most remote parts of the Heaphy Trail. It is known as a good place to see Great Spotted Kiwi, Blue Duck, large snails and large worms. All but the Blue Duck are generally reported as being best seen at night or dawn/dusk. (GPS coords 40.8907S 172.3533E)

The Forest Below James Mackay Hut (site 2) is where I was excited to see a Great Spotted Kiwi and also hear them 4 times. On my trip, kiwi were also mentioned in the hut record books and in person by other hikers. (GPS coords 40.9261S 172.1600E)

Karamea (site 3) is a town that hikers on the Heaphy Trail will pass through. I think it is a good choice for a base if you want to do day walks in Kahurangi forest and have your own vehicle. (If you are reliant on public transport the starts of the walks are a long way away.) Forest day walks include Karamea Gorge Route Track, Fenian Track and K Road Walking Track. The start of the Wangapeka Track runs east from Little Wanganui slightly further south: it is an alternative to the Heaphy Trail for keen hikers looking for remote wildlife possibilities. (The GPS coords for a short estuary walk where a few waders, known as shorebirds in American English, can be seen are 41.2499S 172.1042E.)

I have not visited the sandy Farewell Spit (site 4) but it is said to have a wide variety of habitats that make it good for birdwatching. At the start is Fossil Point which is a good place to see fur seals. The first few kilometres of the spit is a good area for large groups of waders/shorebirds in the summer. There is an Australasian Gannet colony at the end of the spit which is a massive 60km return trip meaning that for many an organised tour is the only way to see it. However, gannets will feed well away from their colony and so good views should be possible all along the coast. (GPS coords 40.5208S, 172.7430E)

Abel Tasman (site 5) is a very popular national park with general tourists. The scenic coastal footpath is reported to be good for wildlife watching.

Wildlife of Kahurangi

As well as the forest and alpine habitats, there are also some sections of coast. There is a breeding colony of fur seals at Wekakura Point that is difficult to access for humans. There are also protected offshore areas to help with fish populations, but again they are not easily accessible for humans!

Kahurangi is one of the few places with a strong population of native New Zealand snails that can be up to 3-4cm across. The shell colour varies depending on the local rocks and they can be very shiny. Their Latin (genus) name is Powelliphanta. Generally they are seen at night when they come out to feed on worms. They can also be seen at daytime when it is raining. It is illegal to keep a shell that is found in the national park.

I spent most of my time here exploring the Heaphy Trail http://www.doc.govt.nz/heaphytrack http://heaphytrack.com so I could reach more remote areas and maybe increase the chance of rarer native wildlife. From Brown Hut to Gouland Downs Hut there is mixed forest with lots of native birds. From Gouland Downs Hut to James Mackay Hut it is more open and other hikers report seeing Blue Duck in the fast-flowing rivers. From James Mackay Hut it is forested again with more native birds. The James Mackay Hut area is where many hikers report seeing Kea. From Heaphy Hut onwards the path runs along the coast.

The Heaphy Trail is a good example of some of the wilder sections of the forest at Kahurangi. People report seeing the Great Spotted Kiwi nearly all the way along the trail. Based on historical weather data that I have looked at, on average approximately 1 day out of 5 will be wet: For example, despite my careful planning to have 2 days in the excellent Gouland Downs section of the Heaphy Trail I was unlucky and had heavy rain on both those days.

On the Heaphy Trail the main sounds I heard were the shriek of the Weka, bubble of the Tui, descending notes of the non-native Chaffinch and the subtler songs/calls of the smaller native birds such as Silvereye, South Island Robin and Rifleman. At night I often heard the Morepork calling. I heard the rolling call of the Great Spotted Kiwi all along the trail after dark and light sleepers often report hearing them at night.

Another walk I considered doing was the Leslie-Karamea Track (which includes the Wangapeka Track) from approximately Takaka to Karamea. This is similar in length to the Heaphy Trail and also passes through lots of forest that could have good birdlife, including Great Spotted Kiwi. One reason it may not be so good is that the anti-predator measures are focused only in certain places, whereas the Heaphy Trail gets very good coverage.

The Golden Bay coast is, according to population data, one of the only places where you can see Reef Heron in New Zealand, so if you are a keen birdwatchers you may want to look out for it. In the wetland areas you might also look out for White-faced Heron, Masked Lapwing, Variable Oystercatcher and Black-winged Stilt.

These are the mammals and field signs that I saw on my 7 day visit: (Almost all seen on the Heaphy Trail.)

possum 3x1 (m2) (non-native) (along the beach)

rat 2x1 (m1) (non-native) (along the beach)

deer tracks (near Lewis Hut where others have seen them)

rat tracks and droppings (along the beach)

hare 1x1 (m1) (along the beach)

Birds that I missed included the alpine/high-elevation Rock Wren, Kea and Blue Duck (all of which are less commonly seen) plus the New

Zealand Falcon (which is generally difficult to find) and the Morepork (which is nocturnal and you need some luck to see it).

Non-native birds I saw on my 7 day visit were Australian Magpie, Starling, Song Thrush, Chaffinch, Blackbird, Greenfinch, House Sparrow, Mallard, Yellowhammer and Californian Quail.

I saw 27 species of native bird:- (I also saw large parrots 4 times that were either Kaka or Kea but I wasn't sure which.)

Great Spotted Kiwi (*Apteryx haastii*) 1x1 (m1)
Paradise Shelduck (*Tadorna variegata*) 5x3 (m4)
Variable Oystercatcher (*Haematopus unicolor*) 8x3 (m5)
Pied Stilt/Black-winged Stilt (*Himantopus himantopus*) 1x1 (m1)
Spur-winged Plover/Masked Lapwing (*Vanellus miles*) 2x1 (m1)
Pied Shag (*Phalacrocorax varius*) 3x3 (m5)
Little Shag (*Phalacrocorax melanoleucos*) 1x1 (m1)
Black Shag (*Phalacrocorax carbo*) 1x1 (m1)
White-faced Heron (*Egretta novaehollandiae*) 1x1 (m1)
Reef Heron (*Egretta sacra*) 1x1 (m1)
Swamp Harrier/Australasian Harrier (*Circus approximans*) 3x1 (m1)
Weka (*Gallirallus australis*) 12x2 (m4)
Purple Swamphen/Pukeko (*Porphyrio melanotus*) 1x1 (m1)
Kelp Gull/Black-backed Gull (*Larus dominicanus*) 6x2 (m4)
Red-billed Gull (*Larus novaehollandiae*) 1x1 (m1)
New Zealand Pigeon (*Hemiphaga novaeseelandiae*) 5x2 (m2)
Rifleman (*Acanthisitta chloris*) 6x2 (m3)
Grey Warbler (*Gerygone igata*) 2x2 (m2)
Bellbird (*Anthornis melanura*) 2x3 (m3)
Tui (*Prosthemadera novaeseelandiae*) 7x2 (m2)
Brown Creeper (*Mohoua novaeseelandiae*) 3x2 (m2)
New Zealand Fantail (*Rhipidura fuliginosa*) 3x2 (m2)
Tomtit (*Petroica macrocephala*) 6x1 (m1)
South Island Robin (*Petroica australis*) 3x2 (m2)
Fernbird (*Bowdleria punctata*) 1x1 (m1)
Silvereye (*Zosterops lateralis*) 8x4 (m12)
Welcome Swallow (*Hirundo neoxena*) 3x2 (m2)

Powelliphanta snails are a highlight of the Kahurangi forest.

Location 2: Paparoa (New Zealand)

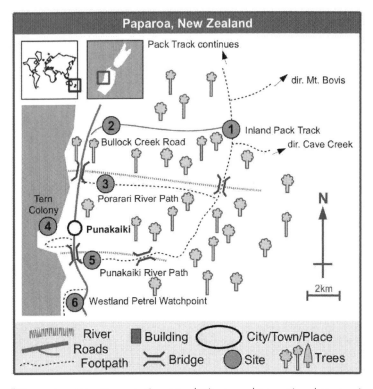

Paparoa, New Zealand

Pack Track continues

dir. Mt. Bovis

Inland Pack Track

Bullock Creek Road

dir. Cave Creek

Porarari River Path

Tern Colony

Punakaiki

Punakaiki River Path

Westland Petrel Watchpoint

N

2km

River · Roads · Footpath · Building · Bridge · City/Town/Place · Site · Trees

*"Forest with Great Spotted Kiwi and Westland Petrel;
Rocky coast with a white-fronted Tern colony."*

My favourite sites were the Inland Pack Track where I saw Great Spotted Kiwi on a night walk and the beach at the Westland Petrel Watchpoint where I saw this rare seabird flying overhead at dusk.

This location description is based on my visit in spring 2016. I found that the Great Spotted Kiwi was not well known by the locals. However, other wildlife-watching visitors have reported them from the same place I saw them and also on the track to Mount Bovis. If you are a multi-day hiker you may be interested to know that I have heard of people wild camping on Mount Bovis and then returning the next day.

When wildlife watching it is tempting to sometimes walk away from the main trails to try for an extra view or see round an obstacle. At Paparoa be wary of leaving the main paths as I heard that the local geology means there can be sink holes.

Site Summaries

The Inland Pack Track (site 1) is a two day tramp. I walked the section at the end of Bullock Creek Road and thought the forest was very good. On a night walk I heard and saw Great Spotted Kiwi. (GPS coords 42.0996S 171.4048E)

You can walk along Bullock Creek Road (site 2) to get to my recommended section of the Inland Pack Track. The road is also an easy walking or cycling surface and I often got easier views of the birds compared to in the forest: so Bullock Creek Road can be a walk on its own. (GPS coords 42.1001S 171.3426E)

Porarari River Path (site 3) is a popular local walk for tourists. I saw some good forest birds here. If you turn south as you reach the Inland Pack Track you can combine it with the Punakaiki River Path to make a circular walk of approximately 10km with a range of habitats and good wildlife possible. (GPS coords 42.1071S 171.3388E)

There is a White-fronted Tern Colony (site 4) on the cliffs. All along the short, circular path there are different views of the cliffs; depending on where the terns are resting, different spots can offer the best views. (GPS coords 42.1154S 171.3297E)

Punakaiki River Path (site 5) has more open habitats compared to the Porarari River Path. The woodland higher up this path was one of my favourite spots at this location. (GPS coords 42.1249S 171.3311E)

You can park at the car park and walk to the beach to reach the Westland Petrel Watchpoint (site 6). If you walk all the way from Punakaiki (as I did) there is an awkward section of road for about 500m which I think needs at least a torch if you will be coming back in the dark. The watchpoint I found is approximately 1km south of the first car park you reach after Punakaiki. Westland Petrel fly over this beach (and over other sections of beach to the south according to local surveys) at dusk from approximately May through to November. I saw them circle over the sea and then fly over my head from about 30 minutes before dusk onwards. During the breeding season they can be seen feeding during the day a long way along the coast, even as far as the east coast of South Island and the south coast of North Island. However, watching for them returning in the evening is a reliable way to see large numbers of them. (The GPS coords for the watchpoint on the beach are 42.1390S 171.3267E.) (The GPS coords for the car park are 42.1296S 171.3284E.)

Wildlife of Paparoa

In the more open areas I saw lots of New Zealand Flax. I saw 2 wild goats by the road and 2 hare on the Punakaiki River Path.

In the forests I saw birds such as Fantail, Weka, Tui, South Island Robin, Grey Warbler and New Zealand Pigeon.

This coast has some fur seals and Little Penguins but I did not find Paparoa to be the easiest nor most reliable place for them. I also preferred to see them at other locations where viewing is more organised or a more common activity so that I could be more confident I was not disturbing them.

On two night-time walks in October 2016 (starting at 2am and walking until dawn) I regularly heard Morepork. I saw possum along Bullock Creek Road, a Stoat along the Punakaiki River Path and heard and saw Great Spotted Kiwi on the Inland Pack Track section I have described as site 1.

I saw 23 species of bird on a 3 day visit in October 2016: (I also saw the non-native Starling, Blackbird, Chaffinch, Song Thrush and Goldfinch.)

Great Spotted Kiwi (*Apteryx haastii*) 1x2 (m2)
Paradise Shelduck (*Tadorna variegata*) 3x2 (m2)
Variable Oystercatcher (*Haematopus unicolor*) 2x2 (m2)
South Island Pied Oystercatcher (*Haematopus finschi*) 1x2 (m2)
Banded Dotterel (*Charadrius bicinctus*) 4x2 (m2)
Westland Petrel (*Procellaria westlandica*) 1x100 (m100)
Little Shag (*Phalacrocorax melanoleucos*) 3x1 (m1)
White-faced Heron (*Egretta novaehollandiae*) 1x1 (m1)
Swamp Harrier/Australasian Harrier (*Circus approximans*) 1x1 (m1)
Weka (*Gallirallus australis*) 9x2 (m2)
Purple Swamphen/Pukeko (*Porphyrio melanotus*) 2x4 (m7)
Kelp Gull/Black-backed Gull (*Larus dominicanus*) 3x6 (m10)
Red-billed Gull (*Larus novaehollandiae*) 6x2 (m3)
White-fronted Tern (*Sterna striata*) 1x100 (m100)
New Zealand Pigeon (*Hemiphaga novaeseelandiae*) 7x2 (m2)
Grey Warbler (*Gerygone igata*) 2x1 (m1)
Bellbird (*Anthornis melanura*) 3x2 (m2)
Tui (*Prosthemadera novaeseelandiae*) 5x2 (m2)
New Zealand Fantail (*Rhipidura fuliginosa*) 4x2 (m2)
Tomtit (*Petroica macrocephala*) 1x1 (m1)
South Island Robin (*Petroica australis*) 1x1 (m1)
Silvereye (*Zosterops lateralis*) 3x3 (m5)
Welcome Swallow (*Hirundo neoxena*) 2x2 (m2)

White-fronted Terns rest on the rocks between fishing trips out to sea.

Location 3: Haast (New Zealand)

"Fiordland Crested Penguin, Yellowhead and other rarer birds."

I enjoyed seeing the Fiordland Crested Penguin at Monro Beach and I was disappointed to only have a brief look for Yellowhead near Thunder Creek Falls as the bus did not stop for long.

This coastline is protected as the Whakapohai Wildlife Refuge. There are regular reports of dolphins, including Hector's Dolphin, near the beach between Ship Creek and Knights Point. (However, I could not find definite numbers for exactly how likely it was to see dolphins.)

The river here has flowed from the direction of Lake Wanaka in the east which is a popular tourist destination.

This location description is based on my visit in 2016 when the impact of non-native predators and disturbance from visitors was thought to have pushed most of the Fiordland Crested Penguins further south. Sightings from the footpaths and viewpoints at Monro Beach and Jackson Bay were less than in previous years. (However, I still saw them at Monro Beach.) There are some good populations further south on islands and isolated peninsulas in Fiordland: This perhaps means the populations at Haast do not receive so much conservation effort as they are outliers and not the main "ark" population.

If you are adventurous there is a popular Department of Conservation campsite at Lake Paringa north of Haast that is said to be very scenic. There are many trails and I considered doing a multi-day hike from Paringa to Haast.

Site Summaries

Many people drive to Monro Beach (site 1). I caught the Intercity bus from Haast and then gambled I could hitch back to Haast, which I managed to do. The walk from the car park to the beach is through woodland where I got excellent views of Bellbirds, Tui and other birds. At dawn and after approximately 3pm people report seeing Fiordland Crested Penguin, particularly between July and November. I got good views from 4pm onwards in October 2016. In January and February the DoC ask everyone to stay a long distance from the penguins as they may be moulting and unable to swim: they can become tired, hungry and begin to look ill but this is natural and if left undisturbed they will recover. (GPS coords 43.7150S 169.2694E)

Knights Point (site 2) is a viewpoint with the possibility of fur seals and dolphins. (GPS coords 43.7163S 169.2252E)

Ship Creek (site 3) is another viewpoint with the possibility of fur seals and dolphins. (GPS coords 43.7584S 169.1490E)

There is a short walk running alongside the road that starts at the visitor centre at Haast (site 4) where I saw Fantail, Silvereye, Brown Creeper and other native birds during my visit. There is also a walk along Haast Beach (that I did not try) and information boards at the visitor centre. A new trail called the Dennis Road Trail was being developed when I was there: it is intended to give the opportunity for tourists to see commoner native birds such as Tui and Bellbird. (The GPS coords for the visitor centre are 43.8609S 169.0458E.)

Fiordland Crested Penguin used be seen at Jackson Bay (site 5) but non-native predators and visitor disturbance is thought to have pushed them further south to more isolated nesting areas. (GPS coords 43.9722S 169.6137E)

Thunder Creek Falls (site 6) is a popular stopping place to see the waterfall. In 2016 the falls marked approximately the northern-most extent of the range of the native Yellowhead bird (based on generally-available population data). Other forest birds such as Yellow-crowned Parakeet can also be seen. You might try walking up the Lansborough Valley to look for Yellowhead or explore other forest tracks nearby. The DoC "Pleasant Flat" Campsite is nearby. (GPS coords 43.0378S

169.3673E) (The GPS coords for approximately the start of the Lansborough Valley Walk are 44.0133S 169.3851E.)

Wildlife of Haast

In the forest typical birds I saw included the Tui, Bellbird, Kaka (occasionally seen high flying overhead) and New Zealand Pigeon. In open habitats I saw lots of Purple Swamphen, Masked Lapwing, Paradise Shelduck and occasionally South Island Pied Oystercatcher. From the beaches and cliffs I saw Australasian Gannet, White-fronted Tern, Caspian Tern and many other seabirds that were too far away to identify. I enjoyed seeing petrels, gulls and terns diving for fish. I also got a brief view of a dolphin.

I saw 25 species of bird on a 3 day visit in October 2016:- (I also saw the non-native Blackbird, Song Thrush, House Sparrow, Chaffinch, Skylark, Mallard, Starling, Yellowhammer, Greenfinch and magpie.)

Black Swan (*Cygnus atratus*) 1x1 (m1)
Paradise Shelduck (*Tadorna variegata*) 6x3 (m4)
Fiordland Crested Penguin (*Eudyptes pachyrhynchus*) 3x2 (m2)
Variable Oystercatcher (*Haematopus unicolor*) 1x2 (m2)
South Island Pied Oystercatcher (*Haematopus finschi*) 3x2 (m2)
Spur-winged Plover/Masked Lapwing (*Vanellus miles*) 6x2 (m2)
Australasian Gannet (*Morus serrator*) 1x1 (m1)
Little Shag (*Phalacrocorax melanoleucos*) 1x1 (m1)
Black Shag (*Phalacrocorax carbo*) 2x1 (m1)
Swamp Harrier/Australasian Harrier (*Circus approximans*) 2x1 (m1)
Purple Swamphen/Pukeko (*Porphyrio melanotus*) 7x3 (m7)
Kelp Gull/Black-backed Gull (*Larus dominicanus*) 9x2 (m5)
Red-billed Gull (*Larus novaehollandiae*) 1x1 (m1)
Caspian Tern (*Hydroprogne caspia*) 1x1 (m1)
White-fronted Tern (*Sterna striata*) 1x1 (m1)
New Zealand Pigeon (*Hemiphaga novaeseelandiae*) 7x2 (m2)
Kea (*Nestor notabilis*) 1x1 (m1)
Shining Bronze-cuckoo (*Chrysococcyx lucidus*) 1x1 (m1)
Bellbird (*Anthornis melanura*) 8x2 (m2)
Tui (*Prosthemadera novaeseelandiae*) 11x2 (m3)
Brown Creeper (*Mohoua novaeseelandiae*) 1x2 (m2)
New Zealand Fantail (*Rhipidura fuliginosa*) 1x2 (m2)
Tomtit (*Petroica macrocephala*) 2x2 (m2)
Silvereye (*Zosterops lateralis*) 1x2 (m2)
Welcome Swallow (*Hirundo neoxena*) 3x2 (m2)

The self-introduced Silvereye can be seen in native forest, parks and gardens throughout New Zealand.

Location 4: Fiordland (New Zealand)

Fiordland, New Zealand

"Mountains by the sea with dolphins, penguins and seals."

I enjoyed seeing a variety of birds at the pedestrian-friendly **Te Anau**. I also found some good places to explore on foot at **Milford Sound**. The Homer Tunnel has accessible, high-elevation trails where other birdwatchers have seen Rock Wren.

Fiordland is a place of dramatic scenery, very wet and relatively remote. There are a few places to visit on the edge, but the national park itself is little-explored. The prevailing winds come from the west and carry clouds off the sea which then rise up the sides of the mountains at Fiordland, causing the high rainfall. The rain creates many stunning waterfalls but can limit wildlife watching.

Places on the edge of the national park, such as Milford Sound and Te Anau, are popular destinations with various-length trails along lake edges and through forest. The forest is reported to be home to South Island bird species including kiwi and Yellowhead. Ferry, aeroplane and helicopter trips offer alternative ways to enjoy the park.

It is possible to explore deep into the national park only if you are an experienced hiker with a few days to spare. The Dusky Track takes you into the heart of Fiordland and very few people walk it. Slightly less adventurous, but still difficult, are the Milford Trail (5 days from direction of Te Anau), Hollyford Track (8 days to the coast and back along the same route) and Routeburn Track (3 days from direction of Queenstown) all of which are near Milford Sound. The Milford Trail is particularly famous for its scenic beauty. The Hollyford Track is known for wildlife, including fur seals and Fiordland Crested Penguin. There are also the South Coast Track and Hump Ridge Track to the south side of Fiordland National Park, which also pass through coastal habitats and rainforest. For all these tracks I recommend that you check with the Department of Conservation http://www.doc.govt.nz/parks-and-recreation/places-to-go/ to confirm any booking requirements.

Driving to Milford Sound requires a long route, with a proposed new road linking Milford Sound and Haast being resisted as it would cut right through a wilderness area. In theory you could hike from Milford Sound to Haast through this wilderness, mainly through Mount Aspiring National Park. You would have to be an incredibly experienced hiker to do this. The Department of Conservation website has details about the network of footpaths that this would involve.

Site Summaries

Sites in bold each have their own chapter later in the book.

Many tourists take a boat cruise at **Milford Sound (site 1)** which gives the chance of seeing dolphins, fur seals and Fiordland Crested Penguin. There are also short walks and, even if you are reliant on public transport, there are a couple of day walks. Population data says that Yellowhead and kiwi live here but I did not see or hear them. (GPS coords 44.6715S 167.9249E)

At **Te Anau (site 2)** you can walk the start of the Kepler Track and/or a lakeside path. There is a bird sanctuary that includes a large enclosure involved with captive breeding and rearing of Takahe; an endangered, flightless bird. (GPS coords 45.4237S 167.7190E)

The Milford Track (site 3) is a famous 4 day hike from Lake Te Anau to Milford Sound.

The Hollyford Valley (site 4) is approximately 4 days hike from the start of the track to the coast and then 4 days hike returning the same way. I have seen it described as better for wildlife than the Milford Track including fur seals along the edges of the lakes and Fiordland Crested Penguin as you reach the coast at Martins Bay.

The Kepler Track (site 5) travels in and around an area of land with predator control. The lake edges made it easier to form a complete boundary which is one reason this protected area was created. This is a good choice of track to hike if you want to see kiwi, parakeets, Rifleman and other native wildlife. (GPS coords 45.4401S 167.6854E)

Tutoko River Walk (site 6) goes through a forest full of ferns. The track is uneven and I would not believe the sign at the start: on my visit I never made it out of the forest! (GPS coords 44.6773S 167.9627E)

The South Coast Track and Hump Ridge Track (site 7) is an alternative area for hiking the edges of the forest to the south of Fiordland.

On the eastern side (the Te Anau side) of the Homer Tunnel (site 8) is the start of a footpath that leads onto the rocky slopes. Sometimes this footpath is closed due to snow or rock falls. Birdwatchers have reported seeing Rock Wren around the start of the tunnel and from the path. (GPS coords 44.7645S, 167.9894E)

Manapouri (site 9) is the access point for Doubtful Sound which, depending on your personal preference, you may like more than Milford Sound. Doubtful Sound is more secluded, larger and typically more expensive to visit. The adventurous Dusky Trail starts here. Day hikes and other activities are available. I met many tourists who said this was their favourite place to visit in Fiordland.

As you drive between Te Anau and the start of the Homer Tunnel, the road passes along the Eglington Valley (site 10). It then reaches a saddle in the mountains before dropping back down into the Hollyford Valley. Other birdwatchers have seen Blue Duck in the rivers here. If you are travelling by public transport I have discovered that seeing them is difficult because the coach doesn't stop in suitable places.

Wildlife of Fiordland

To give an idea of the birds that can be seen while travelling by road, this list shows the 12 native species of bird that I saw on a bus journey that included 3 short stops when we could get out and explore for a few minutes:- (I also saw the non-native species Blackbird, Australasian Magpie, House Sparrow, Yellowhammer, Starling, Skylark, Mallard, Little Owl and Song Thrush.)

Paradise Shelduck (*Tadorna variegata*) 3x5 (m11)

Great Crested Grebe/Australasian Crested Grebe (*Podiceps cristatus*) 1x2 (m2)

South Island Pied Oystercatcher (*Haematopus finschi*) 6x2 (m3)

Spur-winged Plover/Masked Lapwing (*Vanellus miles*) 10x2 (m3)

Black Shag (*Phalacrocorax carbo*) 1x1 (m1)

Swamp Harrier/Australasian Harrier (*Circus approximans*) 8x1 (m1)

Weka (*Gallirallus australis*) 1x1 (m1)

Kelp Gull/Black-backed Gull (*Larus dominicanus*) 2x1 (m1)

Black-billed Gull (*Larus bulleri*) 1x20 (m20)

New Zealand Pigeon (*Hemiphaga novaeseelandiae*) 1x1 (m1)

Kea (*Nestor notabilis*) 3x2 (m2)

Tui (*Prosthemadera novaeseelandiae*) 1x1 (m1)

Epiphytes are plants that live on the trunk and branches of trees. They have evolved to make do with little or no soil. The advantages include being away from many grazing animals and being higher up so that their leaves are hit by more sunlight before the leaves of the tree have captured the light instead.

Site 1: Milford Sound (Fiordland, New Zealand)

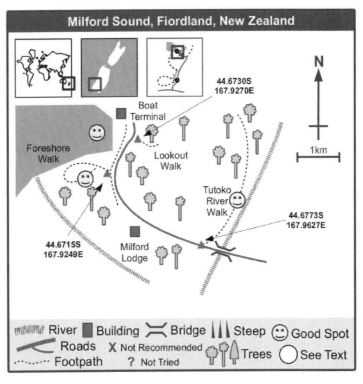

GPS coords 44.6715S 167.9249E

"A forest full of ferns and birds with dolphins on the sound."

I enjoyed seeing the native forest on the **Tutoko River Walk** and looking for dolphins in the water and birds in the trees on the **Foreshore Walk**.

This site description is based on my visit in summer 2016 when I learnt from local residents that rain is very common. I stayed at the Milford Sound Lodge http://www.milfordlodge.com which has dormitory rooms if you want budget accommodation.

Boat trips from the Milford Sound terminal will specifically look for dolphins, fur seals and other wildlife. However, if you are on a budget or just want to go walking, dolphins can still be seen. Many people see them close to shore and I saw 2 for about 15 minutes from the Foreshore Walk.

I did not find the Lookout Walk to be so good as the Foreshore Walk.

The Fiordland Crested Penguin is a famous, rare species that breeds on the south-western coast of the South Island. However, based on reports of other visitors I think you have to take a boat tour to have a realistic chance of seeing them.

If you are staying at Milford Sound the Tutoko River Walk (site 6) can be explored on foot if you do not mind the 3km walk along the road to the start: This is how I managed to do it.

When I visited there was a tourist bus that was not too expensive (but not really cheap either) that could drop you off at the Homer Tunnel in the morning and then pick you up mid-afternoon so if you do not have your own transport site 8 is also possible. I recommend asking at your accommodation if this interests you.

I saw 16 species of native birds during one day of intensive birdwatching on the Tutoko River Walk, Foreshore Walk and Lookout Walk:- (I also saw the non-native Blackbird, Chaffinch and Dunnock.)

Paradise Shelduck (*Tadorna variegata*) 2x2 (m2)
Grey Duck (*Anas superciliosa*) 1x2 (m2)
Variable Oystercatcher (*Haematopus unicolor*) 1x4 (m4)
Little Shag (*Phalacrocorax melanoleucos*) 1x1 (m1)
Black Shag (*Phalacrocorax carbo*) 1x3 (m3)
Weka (*Gallirallus australis*) 2x3 (m4)
Kelp Gull/Black-backed Gull (*Larus dominicanus*) 1x1 (m1)
New Zealand Pigeon (*Hemiphaga novaeseelandiae*) 3x1 (m1)
Kea (*Nestor notabilis*) 2x3 (m4)
Grey Warbler (*Gerygone igata*) 2x2 (m3)
Bellbird (*Anthornis melanura*) 5x1 (m1)
Tui (*Prosthemadera novaeseelandiae*) 2x2 (m2)
Brown Creeper (*Mohoua novaeseelandiae*) 3x1 (m1)
New Zealand Fantail (*Rhipidura fuliginosa*) 3x2 (m2)
Tomtit (*Petroica macrocephala*) 8x2 (m3)
South Island Robin (*Petroica australis*) 2x1 (m1)

The rainforest in the valleys is full of tree ferns and moisture-loving mosses, lichens and liverworts.

Site 2: Te Anau (Fiordland, New Zealand)

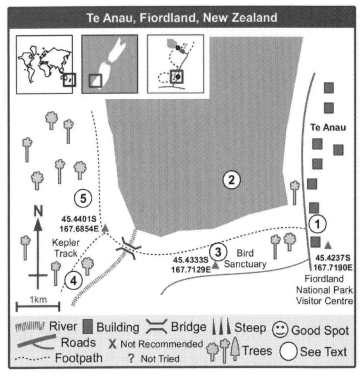

Te Anau, Fiordland, New Zealand

Te Anau

45.4401S
167.6854E

N

Kepler
Track

45.4333S
167.7129E

③ Bird
Sanctuary

45.4237S
167.7190E

Fiordland
National Park
Visitor Centre

1km

River █ Building ⟩⟨ Bridge ⦀ Steep ☺ Good Spot
Roads ✗ Not Recommended 🌳 Trees ◯ See Text
········· Footpath ? Not Tried

GPS coords 45.4237S 167.7190E

"Wild forest birds and a bird sanctuary."

On a short visit I enjoyed birdwatching on sections of the **Kepler Track** and seeing the captive breeding program, including Takahe, at the **Bird Sanctuary**.

Birds that live on the lake include New Zealand Scaup, Great Crested Grebe, Black-billed Gull, White-faced Heron, Little Shag and Paradise Shelduck.

The bird sanctuary has rescue birds and is also involved in captive breeding programmes. This site description is based on my visit in summer 2016 when I really enjoyed seeing the endangered, flightless Takahe: I recommend that you might time your visit to coincide with the morning feed although I personally had luck with visiting late in the evening when it was quiet.

On a half-day walk along the lake from the town and along a short section of the Kepler Track I saw 14 species of native birds:- (I also saw the non-native House Sparrow, Mallard, Blackbird, Starling, Greenfinch, Dunnock, Song Thrush and Yellowhammer.)

Paradise Shelduck (*Tadorna variegata*) 3x4 (m7)
Great Crested Grebe/Australasian Crested Grebe (*Podiceps cristatus*) 1x2 (m2)
Spur-winged Plover/Masked Lapwing (*Vanellus miles*) 1x1 (m1)
Little Shag (*Phalacrocorax melanoleucos*) 1x2 (m2)
Black Shag (*Phalacrocorax carbo*) 1x1 (m1)
Kelp Gull/Black-backed Gull (*Larus dominicanus*) 1x2 (m2)
Black-billed Gull (*Larus bulleri*) 3x6 (m10)
Grey Warbler (*Gerygone igata*) 1x1 (m1)
Bellbird (*Anthornis melanura*) 1x1 (m1)
Tui (*Prosthemadera novaeseelandiae*) 3x2 (m2)
New Zealand Fantail (*Rhipidura fuliginosa*) 3x2 (m2)
Tomtit (*Petroica macrocephala*) 1x1 (m1)
Silvereye (*Zosterops lateralis*) 2x2 (m2)
Welcome Swallow (*Hirundo neoxena*) 1x1 (m1)

The sanctuary at Te Anau had a pair of Takahe when I visited in 2016; this native, flightless bird has a low but stabilised and slowly-growing population.

Location 5: Stewart Island (New Zealand)

Stewart Island, New Zealand

North Circuit Track — 5

Rakiura Track — 4

Codfish Island — 7

Freshwater Hut

Oban — 1

Mason Bay — 3

Ulva Island — 2

South Circuit Track — 6

N

10km

ΛΙΛΛΛΛΛΛΛΛ River	■ Building	⬭ City/Town/Place
Roads		
·········· Footpath	⋈ Bridge	● Site 🌲🌲 Trees

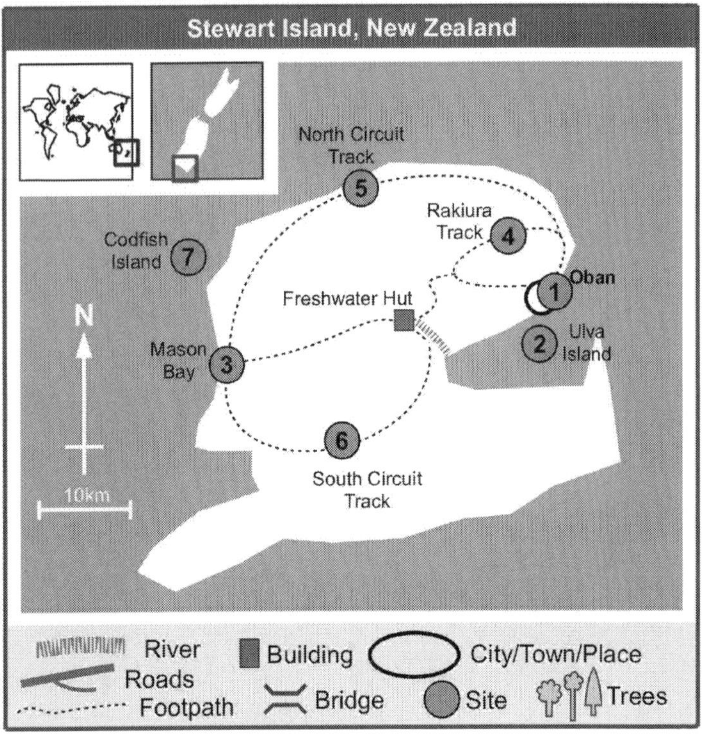

"Less non-native species on Stewart Island means more native wildlife."

I enjoyed looking around **Oban** where I saw plenty of good wildlife. My trip to **Ulva Island** gave me some fantastic views of rarer species of bird.

Stewart Island is a relatively small island (compared to North Island and South Island) that has had less non-native wildlife introduced. This location description is based on my 2 week stay in summer 2016. By comparison with South Island and North Island, I was impressed by the amount of native vegetation (and many other people report the same). In and around Oban are a lot of native birds which survey results suggest is at least partly due to anti-predator controls around the town. There are still some non-native predators, in particular rats, that mean bird numbers are low on the island as a whole.

Away from the fantastic wildlife watching around Oban, the further reaches of Stewart Island can be explored on foot with optional help from water taxis and small planes. There is a regular ferry to Ulva Island. If you have very limited time or find walking difficult you can hire a car from the visitor centre by the quay that can take you to many of the sites in and around Oban (that are more typically explored on foot as the distances are not too great).

Rakiura Charters and Water Taxi http://www.rakiurawatertaxi.co.nz provide an alternative way to Ulva Island (compared to the timetabled service that runs from the southern jetty) that is more expensive but has flexible times and takes a longer route to give some extra wildlife-watching opportunities. They also offer water taxis and planes to Freshwater Bay and Mason Bay: This can remove the hiking through some of the awful terrain before Freshwater Hut or simply save time getting to Mason Bay.

Mobile signal is very bad away from Oban and I can speak from experience when I warn you that: trying to phone for a water taxi if you are already days into a hike is a challenge. It literally took me over an hour wading waist-deep through bog to get signal! You might check in advance for recommendations of where people are currently getting signal on the trails. I got signal about 4km south of Freshwater Hut along the start of the South Circuit, on the south side of a forested ridge.

If you are very keen, the southern part of Stewart Island around Tin Ridge, Deceit Peaks and Fraser Peaks is a wilderness area. Groups of only up to 6 people are allowed to explore this remote area if they are very experienced. This could offer some exciting wildlife watching, although in terms of the number of birds you see I suspect the predator-controlled areas such as Ulva Island will still be better.

Site Summaries

Sites in bold each have their own chapter later in the book.

Active anti-predator controls in and around the town of **Oban (site 1)** brings the mornings alive with the calls of native birds. You can walk to the north, south and east to see Southern Brown Kiwi, Little Penguin, Sooty Shearwater and other wildlife. (GPS coords 46.9257S 168.1303E)

Ulva Island (site 2) nature reserve is free of predators and is an important home to many endangered, native birds. (GPS coords 46.9271S 168.1152E)

The remote sand dunes and woodland of **Mason Bay (site 3)** are mainly visited by long-distance hikers. Southern Brown Kiwi live here and are active during the day. (GPS coords 46.9265S 167.7803E)

Rakiura Track (site 4) is a short, multi-day hike with good-quality path and huts. It is necessary to book in advance.

North Circuit Track (site 5) is an adventurous hike that can take up to 2 weeks around the north of the island. The rewards include lots of chances to see Southern Brown Kiwi and Yellow-eyed Penguins on the northern shore.

South Circuit Track (site 6) is an adventurous hike that takes maybe 5 days. It is very muddy and arguably does not offer many extra wildlife-watching opportunities.

Codfish Island (site 7) is a nature reserve closed to the public that has protected populations of lots of endangered native wildlife.

This gull seemed to be trying to steal a fish from a seal. I took the photograph from Ringaringa Beach near Oban.

Many non-native predators were never introduced or have been eliminated from Stewart Island. Despite this, a large population of rats on Stewart Island is a serious problem for the native birds. Oban and Ulva Island, where there is lots of predator control, are therefore particularly good for birdwatching.

Wildlife of Stewart Island

White-tailed Deer (introduced from North America) were common when I visited in 2016. When alarmed the tail raises and shows the extensive white fur underneath. I saw tracks all over the island and saw an average of one deer every day.

Unfortunately rats are doing well on Stewart Island. I saw an average of maybe one rat a day and also saw their small tracks about once a day. I definitely noticed the difference in places with lots of control measures such as Ulva Island and Ackers Point.

Some people report seeing feral cats, particularly on the longer hiking trails. I saw their distinctive tracks (that do not show claw marks because cats have retractable claws) twice during my 2 week visit to the island.

Stewart Island is a place where you can see New Zealand Dotterel. They breed in various inland spots and so could in theory be seen feeding on the coastline as well. I did not see one during my visit. In practice I have found the beaches in the Auckland area to be a much better place for this species.

If you are happy to do a guided activity (rather than search for yourself) there is a regular kiwi-watching trip in the evening starting at Oban http://www.stewartislandexperience.co.nz that has a very high chance of seeing wild kiwi. They take a boat trip and then a short walk to a secluded beach where kiwi reliably come to feed on the detritus on the shoreline.

When I travelled from Invercargill (on the South Island) to Oban (on Stewart Island) I took the ferry. It was a fast catamaran so time for seawatching was limited. I met people who had travelled on days when the sea was rough and not seen any wildlife.

On my ferry trip to Stewart Island I saw 5 species of bird:- (I also saw the same species from the beaches and clifftops at Oban.) (The White-capped Albatross is often called White-capped Mollymawk by New Zealanders.) (I also saw very similar birds from the ferry on the way back.) (Many other seabirds went unidentified including petrols and possible storm-petrels and possible prions.)

White-capped Albatross/Shy Albatross (*Thalassarche cauta*) 2x1 (m1)
Sooty Shearwater (*Puffinus griseus*) 2x1 (m1)
Spotted Shag (*Stictocarbo punctatus*) 1x2 (m2)
Kelp Gull/Black-backed Gull (*Larus dominicanus*) 1x10 (m10)
Welcome Swallow (*Hirundo neoxena*) 1x1 (m1)

I saw White-capped Albatross from the ferry and also in Oban harbour during my visit.

Site 1: Oban (Stewart Island, New Zealand)

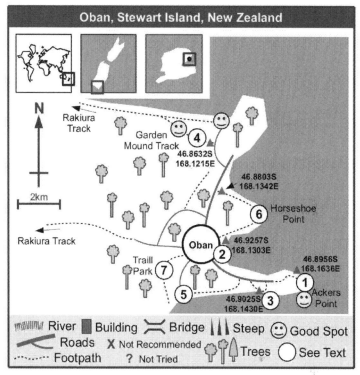

GPS coords 46.9257S 168.1303E

"A small town full of wildlife and wildlife-watching humans."

I enjoyed seeing the Little Penguins and Sooty Shearwater at **Ackers Point** and had fun looking for kiwi on the various **trails to the south of the town**.

Particularly at Ackers Point and Horseshoe Point, the seabirds such as gulls, shags and terns were often too far away over the sea to identify. When you are right on the edge of the sea, I recommend that you listen out for the squeaking of the Little Penguin: this is how I usually saw them.

On my visit in 2016 (on which this site description is based) many people reported seeing a fur seal on a beach or close to shore. I also saw one on a quiet beach in the evening. If you take an organised boat tour fur seals can be much easier to see.

Confused by some tourists for the kiwi, this is a Weka. Stewart Island is one of the best places I have found to see them. Kahurangi National Park also has a strong population.

Here are descriptions of the points marked on the site map:

(1) Ackers Point is home to burrows of Sooty Shearwater and Little Penguin during the spring/summer breeding season. The viewpoint over the cliffs at the end of the path is a good place to watch for albatross, shags and other seabirds. Little Penguins leave and return at dawn and dusk. Unlike some other penguins you are not likely to see them returning during the hours before sunset but instead only at or after sunset. However, Little Penguins often feed close to shore and I saw them in the water during the day. Local residents have being organising predator controls on Ackers Point since 2003 and to me it felt like there were more birds to be seen and the statistics strongly suggest that it helps to protect the Sooty Shearwater and Little Penguin colonies.

(2) The ferry quay is said to be a good place to see Little Penguin at night. Obviously do not disturb them with bright lights or by approaching too close.

(3) Ringaringa Beach, near the golf course, is a good place to look for forest birds, wildlife on the beach (I was lucky enough to see a fur seal here) and in the evening the wide views of the golf course can be good for seeing kiwi.

(4) Garden Mound Track can be a good place to aim for to make an extended day walk starting in Oban and heading north. I saw Red-fronted Parakeets and many other good forest birds in this area.

(5) You can catch the ferry to Ulva Island (site 2) from this jetty.

(6) Horseshoe Point has a scenic walk. In general I did not see so much wildlife here, perhaps because the predator controls are not so good. However, the viewpoint halfway round the footpath (on the clifftop) had some good seawatching where I saw albatross, Little Penguin and other seabirds. On a 3 hour walk I saw the following seabirds: Pied Shag 2x1 (m1), Little Penguin 2x2 (m2), Stewart Island Shag 3x1 (m1), albatross 4x2 (m6), Red-billed Gull 6x2 (m3), Kelp Gull 4x2 (m4), White-fronted Tern 3x2 (m3) and Spotted Shag 3x1 (m1).

(7) Traill Park, along with Ringaringa Beach, was the most-recommended place to see kiwi when I visited. I was not lucky but other people at my hostel saw kiwi in both these places during the 2 weeks that I stayed. Traill Park was generally the most popular place to watch, which I would guess is because it is very close to town so only a short walk.

I saw 24 species of birds during 4 days exploring around Oban:- (I saw an average of 14 different species every day.) (I also saw the non-native Starling, House Sparrow, Blackbird, Redpoll, Mallard, Chaffinch and Song Thrush.)

Paradise Shelduck (*Tadorna variegata*) 2x4 (m5)
Little Penguin/Blue Penguin (*Eudyptula minor*) 4x2 (m2)
Variable Oystercatcher (*Haematopus unicolor*) 9x2 (m4)
South Island Pied Oystercatcher (*Haematopus finschi*) 1x2 (m2)
Sooty Shearwater (*Puffinus griseus*) 2x1 (m1)
Hutton's Shearwater/Fluttering Shearwater (*Puffinus huttoni/Puffinus gavia*) 6x2 (m2)
Little Shag (*Phalacrocorax melanoleucos*) 1x1 (m1)
Stewart Island Shag (*Leucocarbo chalconotus*) 6x1 (m1)
Spotted Shag (*Stictocarbo punctatus*) 7x1 (m1)
White-faced Heron (*Egretta novaehollandiae*) 2x1 (m1)
Swamp Harrier/Australasian Harrier (*Circus approximans*) 1x1 (m1)
Kelp Gull/Black-backed Gull (*Larus dominicanus*) 11x3 (m10)
Red-billed Gull (*Larus novaehollandiae*) 12x4 (m20)
White-fronted Tern (*Sterna striata*) 3x3 (m3)
New Zealand Pigeon (*Hemiphaga novaeseelandiae*) 6x2 (m2)
Kaka (*Nestor meridionalis*) 20x2 (m4)
Red-crowned Parakeet (*Cyanoramphus novaezelandiae*) 7x3 (m8)
Sacred Kingfisher (*Todiramphus sanctus*) 1x1 (m1)
Grey Warbler (*Gerygone igata*) 2x1 (m1)
Bellbird (*Anthornis melanura*) 9x2 (m3)
Tui (*Prosthemadera novaeseelandiae*) 41x2 (m4)

New Zealand Fantail (*Rhipidura fuliginosa*) 2x1 (m1)
Tomtit (*Petroica macrocephala*) 5x2 (m4)
Silvereye (*Zosterops lateralis*) 2x3 (m4)

Kaka, a large native parrot, are common in and around Oban.

Site 2: Ulva Island (Stewart Island, New Zealand)

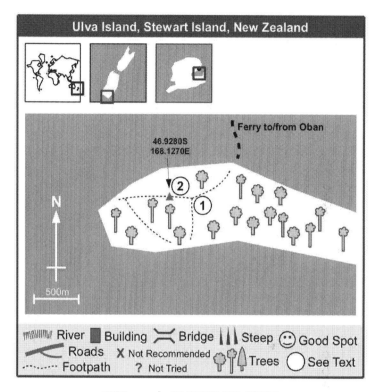

GPS coords 46.9280S 168.1270E

"An island protected from predators that is full of native birds."

I saw good birds all around the island and did not have a particular favourite spot.

There are many non-native, predator-free islands as part of the New Zealand archipelago. Ulva Island is one of the few that is open to the public. A large network of traps occasionally catches a rat that has maybe swum over from Stewart Island or arrived on a boat. Sometimes White-tailed Deer swim over and these are also dealt with. Ulva Island has South Island species which makes it a very different experience to visiting other famous island reserves around the North Island.

In 2016 when I visited (and on which this site description is based), the birds that could be seen on Ulva Island were either much more difficult or impossible to see on Stewart Island. These Ulva-Island-speciality species included Yellow-crowned Parakeet, Yellowhead, South Island Robin, Rifleman and South Island Saddleback.

I had a lot of luck finding Yellow-crowned Parakeet in mixed flocks with Red-fronted Parakeet. Ulva Island was the only place I saw Yellowhead during my whole 2 month trip to New Zealand in 2016. I found South Island Robin to be fairly common in many places and not just Ulva Island. Rifleman is found in throughout South Island and North Island and I found it difficult to see everywhere: Ulva Island was no exception.

Point (1) on the site map is the junction between the three main footpaths on the island. Point (2) is just to the west of the junction where a stream passes the path. During my visit this stream area was the best place for seeing birds, perhaps as it offered a chance for birds to drink compared to many other streams on the island that were dry.

I saw 18 species of birds during 1 day exploring Ulva Island:-

Variable Oystercatcher (*Haematopus unicolor*) 2x3 (m4)
Pied Shag (*Phalacrocorax varius*) 1x1 (m1)
Black Shag (*Phalacrocorax carbo*) 1x1 (m1)
Stewart Island Shag (*Leucocarbo chalconotus*) 2x2 (m3)
Weka (*Gallirallus australis*) 9x2 (m7)
White-fronted Tern (*Sterna striata*) 1x3 (m3)
New Zealand Pigeon (*Hemiphaga novaeseelandiae*) 2x2 (m2)
Kaka (*Nestor meridionalis*) 12x2 (m3)
Yellow-crowned Parakeet (*Cyanoramphus auriceps*) 3x2 (m2)
Red-crowned Parakeet (*Cyanoramphus novaezelandiae*) 8x2 (m3)
South Island Saddleback (*Philesturnus carunculatus*) 4x2 (m2)
Bellbird (*Anthornis melanura*) 4x2 (m2)
Tui (*Prosthemadera novaeseelandiae*) 4x2 (m2)
Yellowhead (*Mohoua ochrocephala*) 1x1 (m1)
Brown Creeper (*Mohoua novaeseelandiae*) 4x3 (m5)
New Zealand Fantail (*Rhipidura fuliginosa*) 5x2 (m4)
Tomtit (*Petroica macrocephala*) 2x1 (m1)
South Island Robin (*Petroica australis*) 11x2 (m2)

Site 3: Mason Bay (Stewart Island, New Zealand)

Mason Bay, Stewart Island, New Zealand

dir. Freshwater Hut

Historical Woolshed

dir. North Circuit

Mason Hut (showing toilet)
46.9265S 167.7803E

(1)

(2) (3) (4)

Historical House

(5)

dir. South Circuit

Big Sandhill

sand dunes

River Building Bridge Steep Good Spot
Roads X Not Recommended Trees See Text
Footpath ? Not Tried

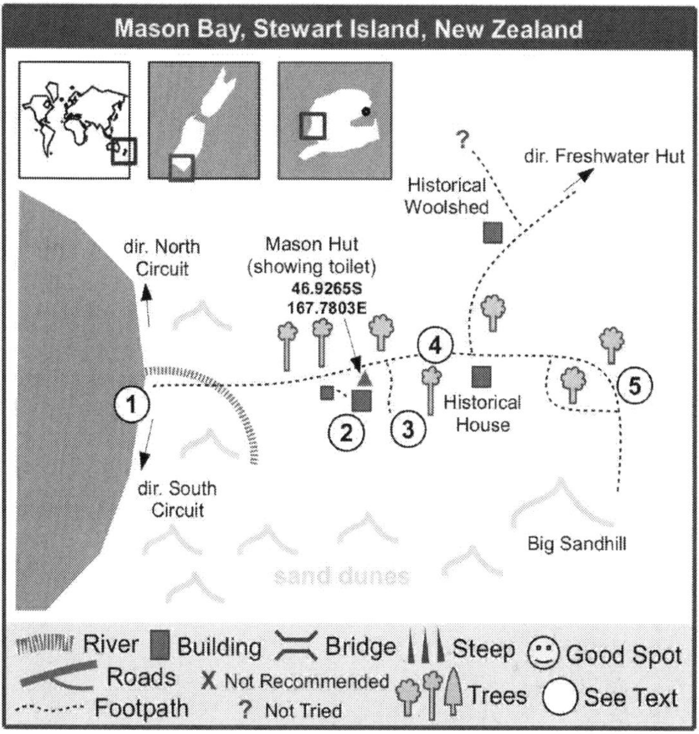

GPS coords 46.9265S 167.7803E

"A beautiful, remote place with dunes and Southern Brown Kiwi."

On my hike I saw a Southern Brown Kiwi near the **path between Mason Hut and the Historical House** which is also where many others have reported seeing them. I also loved the views over the **dune system**.

Mason Bay can be reached by water taxi or plane from Oban or alternatively you can hike from Freshwater Hut. The paths around Freshwater Bay relate to the timber trade. The path between Mason Bay and Freshwater Bay is surprisingly good because it was further improved due to grand plans in the 20th century to develop Mason Bay as a new town (which never happened).

The kiwi in the Mason Bay area are active during the day, giving human a better chance of seeing them.

Sand dunes at Mason Bay appear unspoilt, although there is non-native marram grass that means it looks slightly different to how it would have done before human colonisation.

Here are descriptions of the points marked on the site map, based on my visit in summer 2016:-

(1) There are dunes and beach to the east and south of Mason Bay Hut. The introduced marram grass has partly changed the look of the dunes. It felt very remote and I could not see the kind of damage caused by pedestrians to other sand dunes around the world. If you are a keen botanist you might look for some of the rare species of plant that live in the dunes.

(2) Mason Hut as a well-equipped and free-to-use hut that is very conveniently situated. There are day walks in the local area if you decide to stay for more than one night as I did.

(3) About 100m east of Mason Hut a footpath runs into the bush. This comes out in the sand dunes and at the time I visited it was recommended by the Department of Conservation as a local short walk to then continue east to Big Sandhill. Usually I would be worried about damaging the sand dunes but this is such an isolated place with so few visitors that it does not seem to be an issue.

(4) The footpath between Mason Hut and the Historical House is a hotspot for kiwi sightings.

(5) East of the Historical House there are more footpaths to explore including routes that loop south and back towards the coast. These areas also looked promising for kiwi to me.

I saw 16 species of bird during 4 days in the Mason Bay area:- (This includes some birds seen on the tracks between Oban and Mason Bay.) (I also saw the non-native Redpoll, Blackbird, Chaffinch, Dunnock and Skylark.) (I heard Grey Warbler regularly but as usual they were difficult to see.) (I saw a Southern Brown Kiwi at 9am, well after dawn, about 1km east of Mason Bay Hut.)

Southern Brown Kiwi (*Apteryx australis*) 1x1 (m1)
Black Swan (*Cygnus atratus*) 1x20 (m20)
Paradise Shelduck (*Tadorna variegata*) 2x2 (m2)
Variable Oystercatcher (*Haematopus unicolor*) 1x2 (m2)
Banded Dotterel (*Charadrius bicinctus*) 2x3 (m3)
Swamp Harrier/Australasian Harrier (*Circus approximans*) 1x1 (m1)
Kelp Gull/Black-backed Gull (*Larus dominicanus*) 3x2 (m2)
Red-billed Gull (*Larus novaehollandiae*) 2x2 (m2)
Bellbird (*Anthornis melanura*) 6x1 (m1)
Tui (*Prosthemadera novaeseelandiae*) 3x2 (m2)
Brown Creeper (*Mohoua novaeseelandiae*) 2x3 (m4)
New Zealand Fantail (*Rhipidura fuliginosa*) 1x1 (m1)
Tomtit (*Petroica macrocephala*) 6x1 (m1)
South Island Robin (*Petroica australis*) 3x2 (m2)
Silvereye (*Zosterops lateralis*) 3x2 (m2)
New Zealand Pipit (*Anthus novaeseelandiae*) 4x1 (m1)

This is the view from the path to Mason Bay looking out over a pond within the bog.

Sundew, an insect-eating plant, is found in the boggy areas on Stewart Island.

Location 6: South East Coast (New Zealand)

South East Coast, New Zealand

Oamaru ⑤
Katiki Point ⑥
Mount Cook
Dunedin ④
Sinclair Wetlands ③
Fiordland
Gore
The Catlins ②
20km
Invercargill ①
Bluff
Stewart Island

River · Building · City/Town/Place
Roads
Footpath · Bridge · Site · Trees

"Nesting albatross, shags and gulls plus fur seals."

Combining a visit to **Dunedin** and **Oamaru** in summer 2016 gave me views of large nesting populations of penguins, albatross, shags and gulls. I did not visit The Catlins but others said that Nugget Point was one of the highlights of their stay in New Zealand.

The whole coastline of New Zealand is great for wildlife. On the south-east coast there are a number of seacliffs, promontories and sandy beaches providing homes for a wide variety of bird species.

Based on the reports of other visitors and naturalists, it seems to me that the south-east coast is particularly good for wildlife. Perhaps this is because access to the coast is fairly easy and also there are fewer islands nearby meaning the animals are forced to be on the coast and not offshore.

Some of the cliff-nesting birds are highly protected, or nest in small numbers, making them less visible to tourists. However, there are still large colonies of seabirds easily accessible to wildlife watchers and photographers.

Site Summaries

Sites in bold each have their own chapter later in the book.

Because **Invercargill (site 1)** is where the Stewart Island ferry departs you might find yourself here. I got close views of birds on the lake to the south of the city on my visit in 2016. (GPS coords 46.4196S 168.3373E)

The Catlins (site 2) include the popular Nugget Point and walking tracks such as Catlins River Walk. Bush and wetland habitats give a potentially wide variety of wildlife. Nugget Point is a famous place to see fur seals, seal lions, breeding Australasian Gannet and Sooty Shearwater. Hector's Dolphins are sometimes seen at Porpoise Bay. Yellow-eyed Penguin live all along the coast from Nugget Point to Curio Bay.

Sinclair Wetlands (site 3) is a small wetland nature reserve http://www.tenohoaka.org.nz/ with accommodation that is approximately 20km south of Dunedin on "route 1" (the name of the road). This is considered a good site for more difficult to see birds including Australasian Bittern and Fernbird. (GPS coords close to turning-off point from the main road are 46.0552S 170.0295E.)

Dunedin (site 4) has an albatross colony, fur seals and other coastal wildlife. (GPS coords 45.7762S 170.7293E)

Oamaru (site 5) has Little Penguins nesting in burrows on the slopes above the beaches, Yellow-eyed Penguins at Bushy Beach and a colony of shags in the harbour. (GPS coords 45.1098S 170.9803E)

You can take a short walk at Katiki Point (site 6) to a viewing area for Yellow-eyed Penguin. Yellow-eyed Penguins are typically seen approximately 2 or 3 hours before dusk. I have not been here but others say it is good.

Little Penguins live in burrows all around the coast of New Zealand. They leave tracks like this as they leave their burrows in the morning. The marks made by their feet are on each side and in the centre the marks are from the tail dragging along the ground.

Site 1: Invercargill (South East Coast, New Zealand)

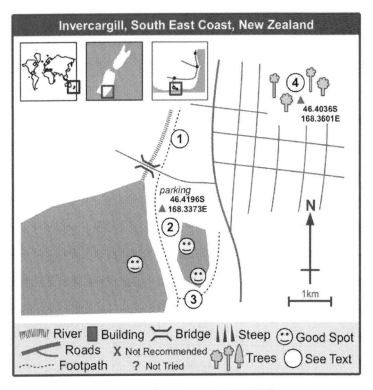

GPS coords 46.4196S 168.3373E

"Black Swan, Australian Shoveler and other birds."

I got some great photographs of waterbirds on the **lake to the south of Invercargill** when I had a day free whilst waiting for the ferry in summer 2016.

There are some small areas of native bush (including within some of the formal gardens) dotted around Invercargill. These are not large, but if you are not visiting good areas of native forest during the rest of your visit then they give some chances of native birds such as Tui and Bellbird.

Further to the south, near the ferry terminal, is Bluff Point Nature Reserve which I have seen described by other birdwatchers as being good for waders (shorebirds in American English) and other waterbirds, particularly in the summer. There is currently a plan to create a cycle path all the way from Invercargill to Bluff.

Black Swan live on the lake to the south of Invercargill.

Here are descriptions of the points marked on the site map (based on my visit in summer 2016):

(1) Kelly Way runs north along the river. I did not see very much here compared to the Estuary Walkway.

(2) The Estuary Walkway runs along by the mudflats and also offers views onto a lake.

(3) Boardwalks run by the lake and create the chance for a circular walk returning either to the parking area or wherever you started in Invercargill.

(4) Queens Park includes a small aviary with a variety of birds including some endangered native species. The iSite at Queens Park has a famous Tuatara conservation programme. The Tuatara are up to about 50cm long, related to the dinosaur and now endangered for the usual reasons due to introduced predators. The breeding here is famous and has played an important role in saving this species of reptile.

I saw Grey Teal on the shore of the lake at the Estuary Walkway and Australian Shoveler on the surface of the lake.

During a 1 day stay at Invercargill I visited Queens Park and the Estuary Walkway. I was reliant on public transport so did not go to

Bluff Point. I saw 15 species of native bird:- (I also saw the non-native Starling, Goldfinch, Blackbird, Song Thrush, Mallard, Greenfinch, Dunnock and House Sparrow.) (Many gulls and ducks went unidentified.)

Black Swan (*Cygnus atratus*) 2x130 (m250)
Paradise Shelduck (*Tadorna variegata*) 2x2 (m2)
Grey Teal (*Anas gracilis*) 1x40 (m40)
Australian Shoveler (*Anas rhynchotis*) 1x100 (m100)
Pied Stilt/Black-winged Stilt (*Himantopus himantopus*) 4x7 (m20)
Spur-winged Plover/Masked Lapwing (*Vanellus miles*) 3x6 (m10)
Little Shag (*Phalacrocorax melanoleucos*) 1x1 (m1)
White-faced Heron (*Egretta novaehollandiae*) 3x1 (m1)
Royal Spoonbill (*Platalea regia*) 1x4 (m4)
Swamp Harrier/Australasian Harrier (*Circus approximans*) 3x1 (m1)
Kelp Gull/Black-backed Gull (*Larus dominicanus*) 5x2 (m4)
Red-billed Gull (*Larus novaehollandiae*) 1x1 (m1)
New Zealand Pigeon (*Hemiphaga novaeseelandiae*) 1x1 (m1)
Tui (*Prosthemadera novaeseelandiae*) 1x1 (m1)
Silvereye (*Zosterops lateralis*) 1x2 (m2)

I saw lots of Grey Teal and Australian Shoveler on the lake.

Site 4: Dunedin (South East Coast, New Zealand)

Dunedin, South East Coast, New Zealand

45.7762S
170.7293E

Dunedin

Portobello

45.8509S
170.6612E

N

5km

🙂︎ River ■ Building ✕ Bridge ┃┃┃ Steep 😊 Good Spot
Roads ✗ Not Recommended 🌳 Trees ◯ See Text
········ Footpath ? Not Tried

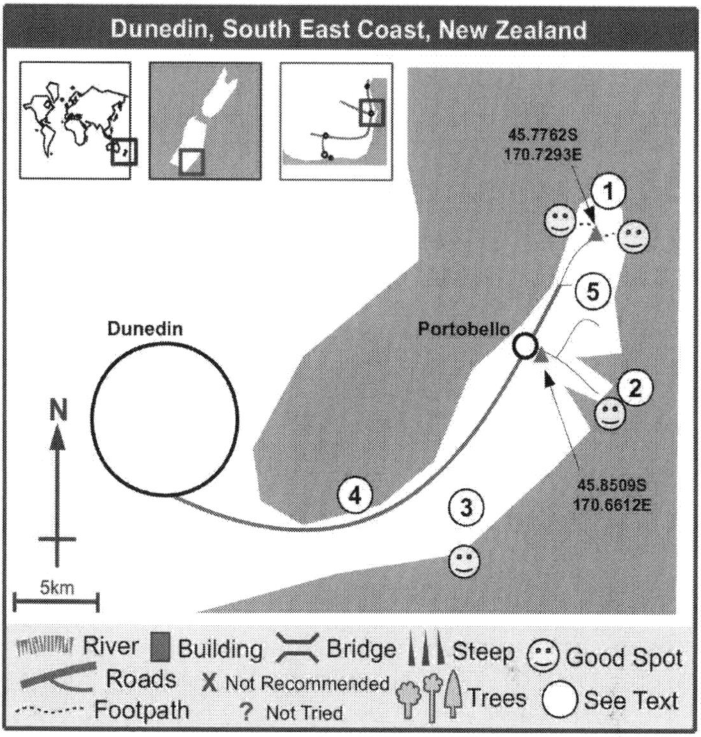

GPS coords 45.7762S 170.7293E

"Albatross, gulls, penguins and fur seals."

I enjoyed seeing the fur seals on the **beach west of Harrington Point** and the albatrosses flying above the sea to the **east of Harrington Point**.

The land east of Dunedin that ends with Harrington Point is called the Otago Peninsula. Harrington Point is also known as Taiaroa Head. Some of the peninsula is closed during September to early November to protect the breeding birds. If you have a car you can keep stopping along the 30km from Dunedin to Harrington Point to look for wildlife. If you are reliant on the public bus then the two sites Harrington Point and Allans Beach fit well with the bus timetable.

Here are descriptions of the points on the site map, based on my visit in summer 2016:

(1) Harrington Point is at the very end of the road. If you catch a local bus then Harrington Point village is the last stop, from where you can walk the last 3km along the road. It is possible to watch the albatrosses, seals and other coastal wildlife from the public footpaths. Alternatively you can pay to go into the Royal Northern Albatross visitor centre which has views in the summer of the nests. You can also pay to get good views of the Little Penguins http://www.bluepenguins.co.nz as they return to the beach in the evening: they can be seen throughout the year. In 2016 the price for seeing the Little Penguins was $30 for an adult with between 10 and 50 being seen every evening.

(2) The road to Allans Beach can be walked from the bus stop at Portobello if you are reliant on public transport. Yellow-eyed Penguin have been seen by other wildlife watchers on the beach. Waterbirds including Sacred Kingfisher and Royal Spoonbill can be seen on Hoopers Inlet that you pass on the way (and also on Papanui Inlet that you might visit with a short drive to the north).

(3) Many small roads and footpaths criss-cross this part of the peninsula. This includes two well-known areas for penguin, fur seal and sea lion: Sandfly Point (30 minutes walk from end of Sealpoint Road) and Boulders Beach.

(4) I did not see very much from the road along the peninsula. If you have a car you might occasionally stop to look at the shags and other birds that perch on the rocks and fly down this section of water.

(5) Penguin Place http://www.penguinplace.co.nz/ is a conservation-themed visitor attraction based around the Little Penguin colony. It has an entry fee and is approximately 3km south of Harrington Point.

On my 1 day visit in 2016 I saw fur seal on both sides of Harrington Point. I saw a group of 12 and a group of 6.

I saw 17 species of native birds on the same visit that included a walk at Harrington Point and a walk partway along the path to Allans Beach:- (I also saw the non-native Goldfinch, Blackbird, House Sparrow, Yellowhammer, Dunnock, Starling, Song Thrush, Redpoll and Mallard.) (Many gulls went unidentified as they were too far away.) (I saw an all-dark-coloured petrel but could not identify it to species.)

Black Swan (*Cygnus atratus*) 1x2 (m2)
Paradise Shelduck (*Tadorna variegata*) 3x4 (m7)
South Island Pied Oystercatcher (*Haematopus finschi*) 1x3 (m3)
Spur-winged Plover/Masked Lapwing (*Vanellus miles*) 1x3 (m3)
Northern Royal Albatross (*Diomedea sanfordi*) 2x1 (m1)
Little Shag (*Phalacrocorax melanoleucos*) 1x1 (m1)
Black Shag (*Phalacrocorax carbo*) 1x1 (m1)
Stewart Island Shag (*Leucocarbo chalconotus*) 5x1 (m1)
Spotted Shag (*Stictocarbo punctatus*) 5x6 (m20)
White-faced Heron (*Egretta novaehollandiae*) 3x1 (m1)
Royal Spoonbill (*Platalea regia*) 3x1 (m1)
Swamp Harrier/Australasian Harrier (*Circus approximans*) 1x1 (m1)

Kelp Gull/Black-backed Gull (*Larus dominicanus*) 5x10 (m20)
Red-billed Gull (*Larus novaehollandiae*) 7x46 (m300)
Sacred Kingfisher (*Todiramphus sanctus*) 1x1 (m1)
Tui (*Prosthemadera novaeseelandiae*) 1x2 (m2)
Welcome Swallow (*Hirundo neoxena*) 3x1 (m1)

Close up there are lots of visual reminders that a fur seal is a mammal.

Site 5: Oamaru (South East Coast, New Zealand)

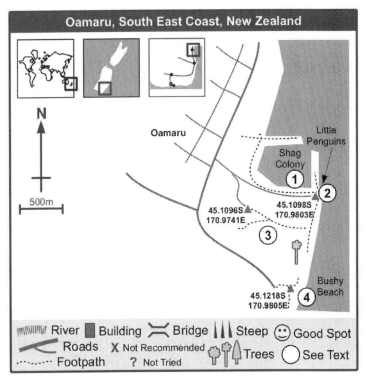

GPS coords 45.1098S 170.9803E

"Seabirds can be seen right next to the town of Oamaru."

My favourite spots were the **shag colony on the pier in the harbour** during the day and **Bushy Beach** where I saw Yellow-eyed Penguins in the early evening.

If you want to see both species of penguin, some people first go to Bushy Beach in the late afternoon to see the Yellow-eyed Penguin. They then move to the Little Penguin colony later, where the action happens close to sunset.

This was a typical view of a Yellow-eyed Penguin when I visited. From the viewing area they can be quite a long way away but this means they are not disturbed and the colony is protected for the benefit of the penguins and also for others to enjoy watching them in the future.

Here are descriptions of the points marked on the site map, based on my visit in summer 2016:

(1) In the summer a shag colony with Stewart Island Shag and Spotted Shag is on a pier by the harbour.

(2) In the evening, just before dusk, Little Penguins arrive. There is an organised viewing area you can pay to go in. Alternatively, some people find a spot by either the road before the viewing area or on the footpath above the cliffs to the south and watch for them swimming, then walking to their burrows. If you are doing it independently remember that you need to move away and avoid them if you happen to be in the way of where they want to go.

(3) There is a network of footpaths on the hill to the south of the harbour. I got some excellent views of seabirds flying close to the paths on the side of the cliff.

(4) Bushy Beach is reached along a road running south from Oamaru centre. There is a viewing area where binoculars can give a good view of (typically) 1 to 5 penguins as they come in to shore during the approximately 3 hours before sunset.

I saw 15 species of native birds on a 1 day visit in November 2016:- (I also saw the non-native Yellowhammer, Blackbird, Chaffinch, Starling, House Sparrow, Goldfinch, Dunnock and Skylark.) (Many gulls, shags and other seabirds went unidentified as they were too far away.) (I also saw 2 skuas which I think were 1 each of Arctic Skua and Pomarine Skua.) (I saw albatross 3 times.) (I saw Spotted Shag, Stewart Island Shag and White-fronted Tern continually all day.)

Paradise Shelduck (*Tadorna variegata*) 2x2 (m2)
Yellow-eyed Penguin (*Megadyptes antipodes*) 4x2 (m2)
Little Penguin/Blue Penguin (*Eudyptula minor*) 1x1 (m1)
Variable Oystercatcher (*Haematopus unicolor*) 2x2 (m2)
Spur-winged Plover/Masked Lapwing (*Vanellus miles*) 1x3 (m3)
Hutton's Shearwater/Fluttering Shearwater (*Puffinus huttoni/Puffinus gavia*) 2x1 (m1)
Australasian Gannet (*Morus serrator*) 1x1 (m1)
Stewart Island Shag (*Leucocarbo chalconotus*) 1x200 (m200)
Spotted Shag (*Stictocarbo punctatus*) 1x300 (m300)
Royal Spoonbill (*Platalea regia*) 4x5 (m8)
Kelp Gull/Black-backed Gull (*Larus dominicanus*) 5x4 (m10)
Red-billed Gull (*Larus novaehollandiae*) 6x5 (m20)
White-fronted Tern (*Sterna striata*) 1x200 (m200)
Sacred Kingfisher (*Todiramphus sanctus*) 1x1 (m1)
Silvereye (*Zosterops lateralis*) 1x1 (m1)

At the shag colony in the harbour I saw birds packed close together. However, the Stewart Island Shags and Spotted Shags kept to separate ends of the pier.

Location 7: Mount Cook (New Zealand)

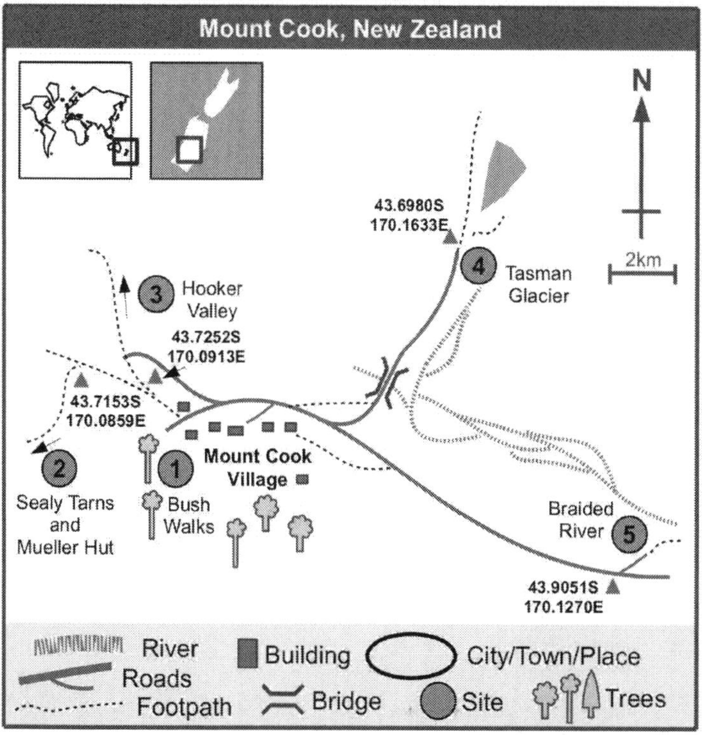

Mount Cook, New Zealand

N

43.6980S
170.1633E

4 Tasman
Glacier

2km

3 Hooker
Valley

43.7252S
170.0913E

43.7153S
170.0859E

2

Sealy Tarns
and
Mueller Hut

1 Mount Cook
Village

Bush
Walks

Braided
River **5**

43.9051S
170.1270E

River	Building	City/Town/Place
Roads		
Footpath	Bridge	Site	Trees

"Spectacular mountains with rare birds in the valleys."

My favourite site was the Braided River but I think I was lucky to see so many birds there. I also enjoyed the many views of New Zealand Falcon on my walk along the Hooker Valley.

If you are happy to see less wildlife, but combine it with mountain views, then Mount Cook is a great place to visit. Obviously in the winter it will be snowy and this location description is based on my visit in summer 2016. Each of the sites might take a day to explore meaning you could stay for 3 or 4 nights and find plenty to do. However, some of the sites are a long walk or require hitching a lift. If you have a car then you might combine them into a series of stops to explore more quickly.

As you go to Mount Cook it passes the Waitaki Valley which is a famous nesting area for Black Stilts. Black Stilts can be seen all around the eastern side of the Southern Alps but in very small numbers.

Site Summaries

All around the main village are Bush Walks (site 1) through areas where I saw and heard Bellbird, Rifleman, Silvereye and other native forest birds in summer 2016.

If you are visiting when most of the snow has melted, the Sealy Tarns and Mueller Hut (site 2) is one of the only chances to get to the elevations where most people reported to me that they had seen Rock Wren. However, there is no guarantee and a local volunteer reported seeing none on transect surveys recently before my visit in 2016. (GPS coords 43.7153S 170.0859E)

In 2016 (and in earlier years) the Hooker Valley (site 3) has been the home of a nesting pair of New Zealand Falcon. It is also a good place to see Mount Cook Lily. (GPS coords 43.7252S 170.0913E)

If you are reliant on public transport the access road to Tasman Glacier (site 4) can be walked as a day walk; I did this and enjoyed the close views of the river valley, unique plantlife and occasional sighting of a bird. Alternatively, if you have a car or hitch a lift, the viewpoint above the car park is just 15 minutes walk to and from the car park. (GPS coords 43.6980S 170.1633E)

To the south is a walk through a section of Braided River (site 5) with typical marshy, pebbly, sandy and muddy habitats. I went through the gate and followed the public track that is used by people going fishing. I was seeing birds all the way along the track as it followed the edges of the airfield. I saw both Black Stilt and Wrybill but was possibly lucky as they are very rare. (GPS coords 43.9051S 170.1270E)

Canterbury Alpine Boulder Copper is a small butterfly found in the Mount Cook area during the summer.

Wildlife of Mount Cook

Non-native wildlife on my visit in 2016 included lots of rabbits, field signs of possum (which was having control measures being introduced so numbers may drop), Canada Geese flying in flocks in the distance across the wide valleys and introduced song birds including Redpoll, Skylark and the particularly common Yellowhammer.

I saw 16 species of native bird during these 3 days at Mount Cook: (This included visits to Tasman Glacier, Sealy Tarns, Hooker Valley and the areas of bush around the village.) (I also saw the non-native Blackbird, Chaffinch, Redpoll, Song Thrush, Dunnock, Canada Goose, Yellowhammer, House Sparrow, Skylark, Greenfinch, Starling and Mallard.)

Paradise Shelduck (*Tadorna variegata*) 3x2 (m2)
South Island Pied Oystercatcher (*Haematopus finschi*) 3x4 (m6)
Banded Dotterel (*Charadrius bicinctus*) 1x1 (m1)
Spur-winged Plover/Masked Lapwing (*Vanellus miles*) 2x2 (m2)
Swamp Harrier/Australasian Harrier (*Circus approximans*) 1x1 (m1)
Bush Falcon/New Zealand Falcon (*Falco novaeseelandiae*) 2x2 (m2)
Kelp Gull/Black-backed Gull (*Larus dominicanus*) 2x2 (m2)
Black-fronted Tern (*Chlidonias albostriatus*) 4x2 (m3)
Kea (*Nestor notabilis*) 1x1 (m1)
Rifleman (*Acanthisitta chloris*) 3x2 (m3)
Grey Warbler (*Gerygone igata*) 2x1 (m1)
Bellbird (*Anthornis melanura*) 1x2 (m2)
New Zealand Fantail (*Rhipidura fuliginosa*) 1x2 (m2)
Tomtit (*Petroica macrocephala*) 1x1 (m1)
Silvereye (*Zosterops lateralis*) 3x2 (m3)
New Zealand Pipit (*Anthus novaeseelandiae*) 1x1 (m1)
On a half-day at the braided river site I saw 11 species:
Black Swan (*Cygnus atratus*) 1x1 (m1)
Paradise Shelduck (*Tadorna variegata*) 3x4 (m7)
Black Stilt (*Himantopus novaezelandiae*) 2x2 (m2)
Banded Dotterel (*Charadrius bicinctus*) 2x2 (m3)
Wrybill (*Anarhynchus frontalis*) 1x1 (m1)
Spur-winged Plover/Masked Lapwing (*Vanellus miles*) 1x2 (m2)
White-faced Heron (*Egretta novaehollandiae*) 1x1 (m1)
Purple Swamphen/Pukeko (*Porphyrio melanotus*) 1x1 (m1)
Kelp Gull/Black-backed Gull (*Larus dominicanus*) 2x2 (m2)
Black-fronted Tern (*Chlidonias albostriatus*) 2x1 (m1)
Welcome Swallow (*Hirundo neoxena*) 1x1 (m1)

If you are lucky you might see Wrybill feeding on the pebbly areas of the braided rivers to the south of Mount Cook. Their curved bill helps them reach for insects under pebbles.

Location 8: Franz Josef (New Zealand)

Franz Josef, New Zealand

dir. Greymouth

N

Whataroa

Waitangitaona
Wetland Walk

5km

Okarito

Franz Josef

Local
Walks

Okarito
Forest

West Coast
Widlife Centre

dir. Haast

River   Building   City/Town/Place

Roads

Footpath   Bridge   Site   Trees

"Glaciers running down into the forest and two sites for rare birds."

The Local Walks east of Franz Josef give views of the glacier and also have native forest birds. In 2016 Okarito Forest was home to the only wild population of Okarito Brown Kiwi and Waitangitaona Wetland Walk offered views of Great Egrets (New Zealand's only breeding colony being nearby).

Site Summaries

At West Coast Wildlife Centre (site 1) the local Okarito Kiwi (also known by other names) are raised in preparation for being released into the wild. By looking after them as they grow up, they are protected during the time that they are most vulnerable to predators. If you pay to go in, there is a fantastic natural habitat where you can watch them. The lighting at the centre is reversed so that it is dark at day and light at night. This means that the usually nocturnal kiwis are active for visitors during the daytime. (GPS coords 43.3877S 170.1830E)

In 2016, surveys indicated that only approximately 500 Okarito Kiwis remained in the whole world. Okarito Forest (site 2) is where they were still surviving. I did not visit when I was in Franz Josef in 2016 partly as I did not want to disturb this rare bird, partly because other kiwis are said to be easier to see in the wild and partly because local conservation efforts means the areas where they are mostly found are protected. (GPS coords 43.2240S 170.1579E)

Waitangitaona Wetland Walk (site 3) runs close to the famous Great Egret colony. For many years this has been the only breeding population in New Zealand. It is a popular bird in local culture. This walk passes through wetland where other birdwatchers have reported seeing the Great Egrets feeding. (GPS coords 43.1799S 170.3683E)

There are a number of popular Local Walks (site 4) east of Franz Josef including one that leads to the glacier (in 2016 when I visited it had not yet melted and maybe had a few years left). Many sections of the path lead through woodland and offer good chances of seeing native birds. (GPS coords 43.3841S 170.1850E)

Location 11: Cook Strait (New Zealand)

Cook Strait, New Zealand

Wellington

N

41.2854S
174.0053E

Picton

10km

River   Building   City/Town/Place
Roads
Footpath   Bridge   Site   Trees

"A ferry between North Island and South Island with some wildlife visible above the water."

I personally enjoyed looking for Fairy Prion on the **central part of the ferry route** when I crossed the strait on the ferry.

If you are visiting New Zealand then you may well take this ferry to travel between the North and South Islands. You may also choose to do a dedicated wildlife-watching trip on a smaller boat: the boats going out of Picton or Kaikoura look excellent to me.

Based on my experience taking the ferry in summer 2016, I think of the route as being in three parts: near the shore, out at sea and then near the shore again. In the deep-sea section I was seeing more of the specialist seabirds such as shearwaters and prions.

Site Summaries

Picton Harbour (site 1) is less industrialised than Wellington Harbour. I saw shags, gulls and other birds; this included Pied Shag resting by the edge of the footpath towards the ferry.

If you are lucky (as I was), and the ferry diverts from the usual route, you might pass the King Shag colony at White Rocks (site 2).

Towards the middle of the Main Channel (site 3) I started seeing lots of Fairy Prion.

Wildlife of Cook Strait

On a 9am crossing from Picton to Wellington in December 2016 I saw 8 species of bird: (I also saw 3 albatross, a dolphin and lots of jellyfish.) (Many gulls, shags, petrels, shearwaters, terns and other waterbirds were either too difficult to identify or too far away to identify.)

Fairy Prion (*Pachyptila turtur*) 7x6 (m20)
Australasian Gannet (*Morus serrator*) 4x2 (m2)
Pied Shag (*Phalacrocorax varius*) 2x4 (m4)
Spotted Shag (*Stictocarbo punctatus*) 4x2 (m2)
New Zealand King Shag (*Leucocarbo carunculatus*) 1x10 (m10)
Kelp Gull/Black-backed Gull (*Larus dominicanus*) 8x2 (m4)
Red-billed Gull (*Larus novaehollandiae*) 2x1 (m1)
White-fronted Tern (*Sterna striata*) 1x1 (m1)

Australasian Gannet nest at only a few places around the coast. When feeding they explore more widely, including into the Cook Strait.

Location 12: Wellington (New Zealand)

"There are some fantastic, protected forest nature reserves near Wellington."

Based on my visit in 2016, my favourite site near Wellington is **Zealandia**. In the future, if the introduced bird populations grow to fill the available space, I predict that I would then prefer **Kapiti Island**.

Site Summaries

Sites in bold each have their own chapter later in the book.

A predator-proof fence protects the **Zealandia (site 1)** nature reserve. It was one of the best places I visited in 2016 for seeing Red-fronted Parakeet, Kaka and Stitchbird, perhaps due to the bird feeders. I saw a wide variety of native forest birds and water birds including Brown Teal and Takahe on my one day visit. (GPS coords 41.2887S 174.7540E)

Kapiti Island (site 2) is a large island that is being kept predator-free. I was impressed by the size of the island on my visit in 2016. An ecotourism lodge is available on the island meaning you can stay overnight. (GPS coords 40.8533S 174.9350E)

Red Rocks (site 3) is a fur seal colony with other coastal wildlife as well. I have not visited but have read reports from others. You can apparently catch the number 1 bus from Wellington to Island Bay, get off at the last stop and then walk a further 2km around the coast to Red Rocks.

I photographed this New Zealand Pigeon sheltering from the rain on Kapiti Island.

Site 1: Zealandia (Wellington, New Zealand)

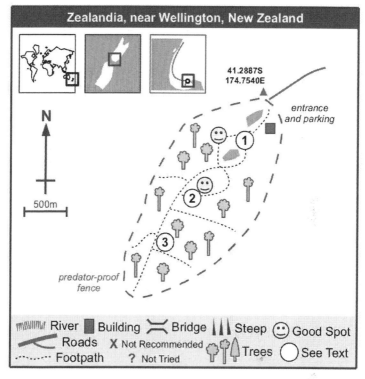

GPS coords 41.2887S 174.7540E

"A nature reserve with native birds and reptiles."

I enjoyed seeing the Tuatara on the **path after the visitor centre** and the native birds on the **feeders in the northern part of the reserve**.

This site description is based on my visit in summer 2016. After the entrance I found some easy trails with a number of feeders and lots of birds to be seen (position 1 on map). This first section also had good places to see Tuatara (reptiles), weta (insects) and geckos. I recommend walking slowly along the Tuatara path and looking carefully in the undergrowth.

After the second lake the trails get rougher and I saw similar birds but fewer people: so sometimes it was easier to take photographs (position 2 on the map). I did not try it but you can explore even further south (position 3 on the map).

Along the footpaths there were often weta boxes which I could look inside of. I also managed to see a weta (that was not in a weta box) in the forest near position 2 on the map.

On my visit I saw 19 species of native bird:- (I also saw the non-native species California Quail, Mallard, Blackbird, House Sparrow and Dunnock.)

Paradise Shelduck (*Tadorna variegata*) 1x6 (m6)
Grey Teal (*Anas gracilis*) 1x1 (m1)
Brown Teal (*Anas chlorotis*) 3x2 (m2)
New Zealand Scaup (*Aythya novaeseelandiae*) 2x2 (m2)
Little Black Shag (*Phalacrocorax sulcirostris*) 1x5 (m5)
Pied Shag (*Phalacrocorax varius*) 1x20 (m20)
Little Shag (*Phalacrocorax melanoleucos*) 1x1 (m1)
South Island Takake (*Porphyrio hochstetteri*) 1x2 (m2)
New Zealand Pigeon (*Hemiphaga novaeseelandiae*) 3x2 (m3)
Kaka (*Nestor meridionalis*) 4x3 (m5)
Red-crowned Parakeet (*Cyanoramphus novaezelandiae*) 2x3 (m3)
North Island Saddleback (*Philesturnus rufusater*) 11x2 (m3)
Stitchbird (*Notiomystis cincta*) 6x3 (m4)
Grey Warbler (*Gerygone igata*) 3x1 (m1)
Bellbird (*Anthornis melanura*) 1x3 (m3)
Tui (*Prosthemadera novaeseelandiae*) 12x2 (m3)
Whitehead (*Mohoua albicilla*) 4x3 (m6)
New Zealand Fantail (*Rhipidura fuliginosa*) 3x1 (m1)
North Island Robin (*Petroica longipes*) 6x1 (m1)

Site 2: Kapiti Island (Wellington, New Zealand)

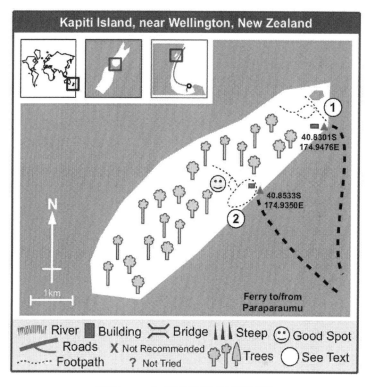

GPS coords 40.8533S 174.9350E

"A large island with a large Little Spotted Kiwi population."

I found the **central part of the island** (position 2 on the map) was the best for seeing wildlife.

You can stay overnight on Kapiti Island http://www.kapitiisland.com and give yourself a good chance of seeing Little Spotted Kiwi either after dusk or before dawn.

This site description is based on two visits in summer 2016. I visited both parts of the island but in retrospect I think you only need to visit the central part (position 2 on the map) to get most of the experience. If you are only visiting for the day I do not recommend also visiting the top part of the island. In theory the lake and wetland to the north could be good but I did not see much there. The only exception to this recommendation is if you are staying overnight because the northern part is where the accommodation is and in that case there is still some good birdwatching to be done if you are there anyway. If staying overnight they seem to drop you off in the central section for the day and then take you to the northern section for the evening.

Interestingly, the Little Spotted Kiwi population has little genetic variability because all today's birds are descendants of just five birds that were taken to Kapiti Island in the early 20th century. Little Spotted Kiwi then became endangered on the mainland while it did very well on Kapiti Island. This strong population of kiwi is one of the key reasons why Kapiti Island is so important.

The island has now been cleared of all pests except mice. Reintroductions of other forest birds are happening to create protected populations of more species. As the years go by, the populations are growing: For example, if you visit after I did in 2016 you should have an improved chance of seeing Kokako (which I did not see) as this species was only a recent introduction. The wardens recommend listening for their beautiful and distinctive fluting call.

I saw only a few Skylark, Yellowhammer and Starling on Kapiti Island and no other non-native birds.

On my 1 day visit to the northern part of the island I saw 21 species of native bird:-

Black Swan (*Cygnus atratus*) 1x6 (m6)
Paradise Shelduck (*Tadorna variegata*) 3x3 (m3)
Variable Oystercatcher (*Haematopus unicolor*) 1x1 (m1)
Pied Stilt/Black-winged Stilt (*Himantopus himantopus*) 1x2 (m2)
Pied Shag (*Phalacrocorax varius*) 3x6 (m10)
Black Shag (*Phalacrocorax carbo*) 1x1 (m1)
Royal Spoonbill (*Platalea regia*) 1x3 (m3)
Swamp Harrier/Australasian Harrier (*Circus approximans*) 1x1 (m1)
Weka (*Gallirallus australis*) 3x1 (m1)
South Island Takake (*Porphyrio hochstetteri*) 1x1 (m1)
Kelp Gull/Black-backed Gull (*Larus dominicanus*) 9x15 (m50)
Red-billed Gull (*Larus novaehollandiae*) 1x2 (m2)
New Zealand Pigeon (*Hemiphaga novaeseelandiae*) 12x2 (m3)
Kaka (*Nestor meridionalis*) 2x1 (m1)
Red-crowned Parakeet (*Cyanoramphus novaezelandiae*) 6x2 (m3)
Bellbird (*Anthornis melanura*) 8x2 (m2)
Tui (*Prosthemadera novaeseelandiae*) 11x2 (m2)
Whitehead (*Mohoua albicilla*) 10x2 (m2)
New Zealand Fantail (*Rhipidura fuliginosa*) 9x2 (m2)
North Island Robin (*Petroica longipes*) 5x2 (m2)
Welcome Swallow (*Hirundo neoxena*) 2x1 (m1)

On my 1 day visit to the central part of the island I saw 17 species of native bird:- (This was less than on the northern part of the island but the numbers of the native forest birds were much better which meant I enjoyed it more.)

Variable Oystercatcher (*Haematopus unicolor*) 2x3 (m3)

Australasian Gannet (*Morus serrator*) 1x1 (m1)
Weka (*Gallirallus australis*) 5x1 (m1)
South Island Takake (*Porphyrio hochstetteri*) 1x2 (m2)
Kelp Gull/Black-backed Gull (*Larus dominicanus*) 1x40 (m40)
Red-billed Gull (*Larus novaehollandiae*) 1x1 (m1)
New Zealand Pigeon (*Hemiphaga novaeseelandiae*) 3x2 (m3)
Kaka (*Nestor meridionalis*) 5x2 (m3)
Red-crowned Parakeet (*Cyanoramphus novaezelandiae*) 5x3 (m3)
North Island Saddleback (*Philesturnus rufusater*) 3x3 (m3)
Stitchbird (*Notiomystis cincta*) 4x2 (m3)
Bellbird (*Anthornis melanura*) 12x2 (m3)
Tui (*Prosthemadera novaeseelandiae*) 19x2 (m2)
Whitehead (*Mohoua albicilla*) 6x2 (m3)
New Zealand Fantail (*Rhipidura fuliginosa*) 2x2 (m2)
North Island Robin (*Petroica longipes*) 10x2 (m2)
New Zealand Pipit (*Anthus novaeseelandiae*) 1x1 (m1)

A common bird throughout New Zealand, I saw lots of Tui on Kapiti Island.

Location 14: Auckland (New Zealand)

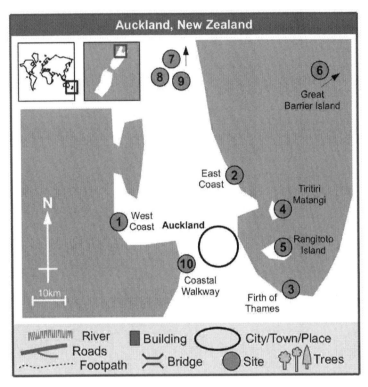

"There are good coastal and forest nature reserves near Auckland."

The gannet colony on the **West Coast** is popular with wildlife watchers and general tourists. **Tiritiri Matangi** is a famous nature reserve that is commonly recommended for seeing native birds.

Within the city, the "Coast to Coast Walkway" (information easily available from tourist information centres) is a walk that other birdwatchers recommend.

To the east, the Hauraki Gulf has whales and dolphins and many seabirds. There are seawatching cruises you can take or you can simply watch the sea when taking a ferry, perhaps when visiting Tiritiri Matangi or another island.

Site Summaries

Sites in bold each have their own chapter later in the book.

On the **West Coast (site 1)** are a gannet colony, a beach walk with New Zealand Dotterel in the summer, forest walks and a marshland that could be good early in the morning. (GPS coords 36.8325S 174.4251E)

There are three stops along the **East Coast (site 2)** near Auckland. This includes a nesting place of the rare Fairy Tern, rock pools, a snorkelling area and a native forest on a peninsula protected by a predator-proof fence. (GPS coords 36.3784S 174.8182E)

On the coast to the south-east of Auckland is the **Firth of Thames (site 3)**. Wetland birds, especially migrant waders (shorebirds in American English), can be seen during the New Zealand summer. (GPS coords 37.1829S 155.3210E)

Tiritiri Matangi (site 4) is perhaps the most famous protected nature reserve in New Zealand. On my visit in 2016 I saw more native, forest birds here than anywhere else on the rest of my 2 month trip. There is basic bunkhouse accommodation available if you want to stay overnight. (GPS coords 36.6067S 174.8932E)

Rangitoto Island (site 5) does not have such a wide range of birds as other islands. I have heard of keen birdwatchers who visit to see Shore Plover on the beaches.

Great Barrier Island (site 6) is 50km offshore and the native wildlife has (as is typical) survived better than on the mainland. The 4-5 hour ferry is an opportunity to do some seawatching. I have not visited but researched the following information: Taking the ferry to Port Fitzroy means you arrive near Okiwi Reserve which is excellent for forest birds and also gives quick access to the trails that head south towards Mount Hobson. Even if you do not have a car, you can explore for 1 or 2 days. Black Petrel nest on the slopes of Mount Hobson and at dusk they can be seen flying back to their burrows. The DoC offers campsites near Port Fitzroy for budget wildlife watchers who want to stay overnight.

Bay of Islands (site 7) is a popular wildlife-watching site that is particularly known for dolphins and waders/shorebirds. Bottlenose Dolphins are seen all year round. I have heard of people seeing whales in the winter.

Puketi and Omahuta Forests (site 8) are connected; together they form a large forest. There are hiking trails with some good wildlife to see including Northern Brown Kiwi (which population data suggests is found in many well-managed forests on North Island).

At the very north of the island are the dunes and specialist wildlife of Ninety Mile Beach (site 9) which has hiking trails.

The **Coastal Walkway (site 10)** offers a long footpath along the coast with waders/shorebirds and other waterbirds. It can also be visited as one or more stops in a car. (GPS coords 36.9460S 174.7613E)

Wildlife of Auckland

Fairy Tern in New Zealand http://www.fairytern.org.nz/ http://www.doc.govt.nz/nature/native-animals/birds/birds-a-z/nz-fairy-tern-tara-iti/ are limited to the Auckland area. They use only a handful of breeding sites including Pakiri Beach and Papakanui Spit. Their New Zealand population in 2016 was approximately 40 (an increase from 10 in the 1983). There are large populations of Fairy Tern in other countries so this is only locally rare.

On the ferry to and from Tiritiri Matangi island in summer 2016 I saw 10 species of native bird:- (Many gulls, terns, skuas and shearwaters went unidentified.)

Little Penguin/Blue Penguin (*Eudyptula minor*) 1x1 (m1)
Variable Oystercatcher (*Haematopus unicolor*) 1x2 (m2)
Spur-winged Plover/Masked Lapwing (*Vanellus miles*) 1x1 (m1)
White-faced Storm Petrel (*Pelagodroma marina*) 1x3 (m3)
Australasian Gannet (*Morus serrator*) 5x2 (m2)
Pied Shag (*Phalacrocorax varius*) 2x2 (m2)
Kelp Gull/Black-backed Gull (*Larus dominicanus*) 5x6 (m20)
Red-billed Gull (*Larus novaehollandiae*) 2x1 (m1)
Caspian Tern (*Hydroprogne caspia*) 2x1 (m1)
White-fronted Tern (*Sterna striata*) 1x1 (m1)

Bird species that nest on islands off the coast of Auckland include: Black-winged Petrel, Cook's Petrel, Pycroft's Petrel, Fairy Prion, Buller's Shearwater, Flesh-footed Shearwater, Fluttering Shearwater, Little Shearwater, New Zealand Storm Petrel, Common Diving-Petrel, Grey Ternlet.

New Zealand Dotterel can be seen at many of the coastal sites around Auckland. This bird is reaching forward and feeling the surface of the sand with one leg to feel for the vibration of small animals that it might then eat.

Site 1: West Coast (Auckland, New Zealand)

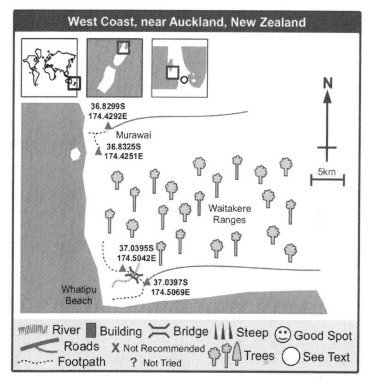

GPS coords 36.8325S 174.4251E

"Coastal wildlife including a large Australasian Gannet colony."

I particularly enjoyed seeing the **gannet colony at Muriwai**.

The Waitakere Ranges have an "Ark in the Park" project in the northern part of the forest. This site description is based on my visit in summer 2016 when I did not visit the Waitakere Ranges because it would have added too much driving and I had already visited many forest reserves elsewhere. I did hear about a visitor centre that is on the road called "Scenic Drive" running west of the town of Titirangi.

Muriwai is known as a place to come and see the Australasian Gannet colony. There are a series of viewpoints on the cliffs looking out over the nesting birds in the spring and summer. Towards the end of summer the young birds will have flown the nest. I also saw White-fronted Terns flying in and around the colony.

Whatipu Beach is a long drive of almost an hour down a one-way road. The reward is an area of native forest, a beach with New Zealand Dotterel in the summer and a marshland behind the beach which is said to be home to rarer wetland birds such as Fernbird. However, I did not see any Fernbird, bittern or other specialist wetland birds on my visit and birds like this are generally difficult to see. In general I would not recommend coming to Whatipu Beach unless you are particularly keen and maybe have the time and fitness to do some walking into the forest. Alternatively, dedicated birdwatchers might make the effort to come here at dawn to make a really good effort for rarer marsh birds. There is a campsite here which could help with an early start and could even make this a nice overnight spot for a holiday itinerary.

I saw 20 species of native bird on a one day visit in summer 2016:- (I also saw the non-native Blackbird, Myna Bird, Yellowhammer, Goldfinch, California Quail, House Sparrow, Chaffinch, Dunnock, Dunnock, Song Thrush and rosella.)

Black Swan (*Cygnus atratus*) 1x2 (m2)
Paradise Shelduck (*Tadorna variegata*) 3x3 (m4)
South Island Pied Oystercatcher (*Haematopus finschi*) 1x15 (m15)
Pied Stilt/Black-winged Stilt (*Himantopus himantopus*) 2x3 (m4)
New Zealand Dotterel (*Charadrius obscurus*) 1x5 (m5)
Spur-winged Plover/Masked Lapwing (*Vanellus miles*) 2x5 (m8)
Australasian Gannet (*Morus serrator*) 1x500 (m500)
Little Black Shag (*Phalacrocorax sulcirostris*) 1x1 (m1)
White-faced Heron (*Egretta novaehollandiae*) 3x1 (m1)
Swamp Harrier/Australasian Harrier (*Circus approximans*) 3x1 (m1)
Purple Swamphen/Pukeko (*Porphyrio melanotus*) 3x3 (m5)
Kelp Gull/Black-backed Gull (*Larus dominicanus*) 5x2 (m2)
Red-billed Gull (*Larus novaehollandiae*) 3x2 (m2)
White-fronted Tern (*Sterna striata*) 1x10 (m10)
Sacred Kingfisher (*Todiramphus sanctus*) 3x1 (m1)
Grey Warbler (*Gerygone igata*) 1x2 (m2)
Tui (*Prosthemadera novaeseelandiae*) 2x1 (m1)
New Zealand Fantail (*Rhipidura fuliginosa*) 1x1 (m1)
Silvereye (*Zosterops lateralis*) 4x4 (m6)
Welcome Swallow (*Hirundo neoxena*) 4x3 (m5)

Australasian Gannets nest at only a few colonies around the coast of New Zealand.

Site 2: East Coast (Auckland, New Zealand)

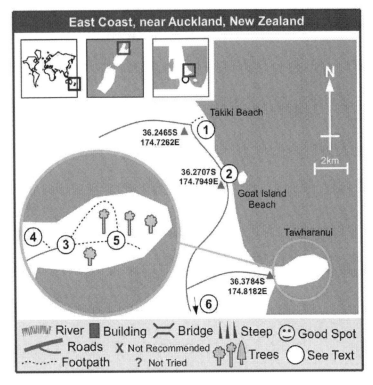

GPS coords 36.3784S 174.8182E

"Beach, rock pools and forest."

I particularly enjoyed exploring **Tawharanui Open Sanctuary** for native birds.

If you are a keen birdwatcher a telescope can be useful for getting better views of seabirds. On my visit in summer 2016 (on which this site description is based) I saw a raft of birds including shearwaters offshore at Goat Island Beach; through binoculars they were too far away to see clearly.

I saw these Variable Oystercatcher feeding alongside rock pools at Goat Island Beach.

Here are descriptions of the points marked on the site map:

(1) Takiki Beach is one of the last remaining breeding areas for Fairy Tern in New Zealand: I was lucky enough to see one fly overhead during my visit.

(2) Wildlife seen at Goat Island Beach included sea urchin, small fish, hermit crab and Neptune's Necklace (a type of seaweed). There are rock pools on the beach and snorkelling gear can be hired to explore the sea between the island and mainland either independently or with a guide.

(3) Tawharanui Open Sanctuary http://www.tossi.org.nz/ is a peninsula cut off by a fence to created a protected area for native wildlife. 2009 saw the first kiwi chicks born on the peninsula with a slowly growing population since then. I think this is a great place to visit with shorter and longer walks available.

(4) I saw a wide variety of forest birds on the Ecology Trail. Brown Teal were feeding along the river next to Fishermans Track.

(5) The Mangatawhiri Track goes through a small wetland. As with elsewhere in New Zealand, I did not see a lot of wetland birds but I did see damselflies and dragonflies.

(6) Below the bottom of the map, towards Auckland, is Wenderholm Regional Park. The forest is not so well protected from predators so all I saw on a visit in 2016 were Tui, Bellbird and Grey Warbler and none of the more sensitive native birds. The beach at Wenderholm has New Zealand Dotterel breeding in early summer and they can be seen feeding at other times of the year.

On a 1 day visit in summer 2016 I saw 28 species of native birds:- (I also saw the non-native Myna Bird, House Sparrow, Yellowhammer, Starling, Mallard, Song Thrush, Australian Magpie, rosella and California Quail.) (I also saw many gulls and shearwaters out at sea.)

Paradise Shelduck (*Tadorna variegata*) 4x3 (m4)
Brown Teal (*Anas chlorotis*) 4x3 (m3)
Bar-tailed Godwit (*Limosa lapponica*) 1x6 (m6)
Variable Oystercatcher (*Haematopus unicolor*) 10x3 (m8)
Pied Stilt/Black-winged Stilt (*Himantopus himantopus*) 1x4 (m4)
New Zealand Dotterel (*Charadrius obscurus*) 3x4 (m10)
Spur-winged Plover/Masked Lapwing (*Vanellus miles*) 2x2 (m2)
Australasian Gannet (*Morus serrator*) 2x2 (m3)
Pied Shag (*Phalacrocorax varius*) 4x5 (m8)
Little Shag (*Phalacrocorax melanoleucos*) 1x1 (m1)
White-faced Heron (*Egretta novaehollandiae*) 4x1 (m1)
Purple Swamphen/Pukeko (*Porphyrio melanotus*) 12x6 (m26)
Kelp Gull/Black-backed Gull (*Larus dominicanus*) 4x2 (m3)
Red-billed Gull (*Larus novaehollandiae*) 5x4 (m8)
Fairy Tern (*Sternula nereis*) 1x1 (m1)
Caspian Tern (*Hydroprogne caspia*) 2x2 (m2)
White-fronted Tern (*Sterna striata*) 3x10 (m20)
New Zealand Pigeon (*Hemiphaga novaeseelandiae*) 6x2 (m2)

Kaka (*Nestor meridionalis*) 1x2 (m2)
Sacred Kingfisher (*Todiramphus sanctus*) 5x1 (m1)
North Island Saddleback (*Philesturnus rufusater*) 1x2 (m2)
Grey Warbler (*Gerygone igata*) 2x2 (m3)
Bellbird (*Anthornis melanura*) 6x2 (m2)
Tui (*Prosthemadera novaeseelandiae*) 19x2 (m3)
Whitehead (*Mohoua albicilla*) 4x1 (m1)
New Zealand Fantail (*Rhipidura fuliginosa*) 3x2 (m2)
North Island Robin (*Petroica longipes*) 1x1 (m1)
Welcome Swallow (*Hirundo neoxena*) 6x2 (m4)

Neptune's Necklace is a common seaweed in and around the rock pools.

Site 3: Firth of Thames (Auckland, New Zealand)

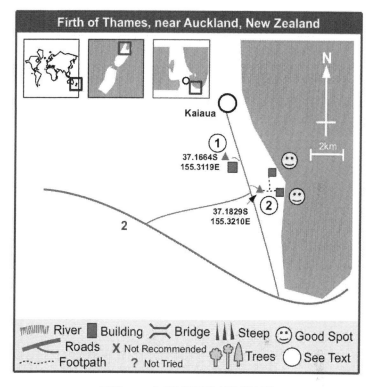

GPS coords 37.1829S 155.3210E

"There are waders/shorebirds all year with the best views reported at high tide in summmer."

I saw the most birds from the **hides overlooking the sea at position 2**.

A good place to start is the Miranda Shorebird Centre http://www.miranda-shorebird.org.nz which has a sightings board showing what other people have seen and information about the trails and hides in the area. There is accommodation at the centre but I think that unless you are very keen on wader watching (waders are known as shorebirds in American English) there is not enough other wildlife interest for a long visit.

I saw 16 species of native bird on a half-day visit in summer 2016:- (I saw large groups of waders/shorebirds and gulls in the distance that I could not identify.)

Paradise Shelduck (*Tadorna variegata*) 1x1 (m1)
Knot (*Calidris canutus*) 2x7 (m8)
Bar-tailed Godwit (*Limosa lapponica*) 3x17 (m30)
Variable Oystercatcher (*Haematopus unicolor*) 1x2 (m2)
South Island Pied Oystercatcher (*Haematopus finschi*) 3x5 (m5)
Pied Stilt/Black-winged Stilt (*Himantopus himantopus*) 2x6 (m10)
Pacific Golden Plover (*Pluvialis fulva*) 1x2 (m2)
Wrybill (*Anarhynchus frontalis*) 2x4 (m7)
Spur-winged Plover/Masked Lapwing (*Vanellus miles*) 2x3 (m3)
Pied Shag (*Phalacrocorax varius*) 1x2 (m2)
White-faced Heron (*Egretta novaehollandiae*) 2x21 (m40)
Swamp Harrier/Australasian Harrier (*Circus approximans*) 2x1 (m1)
Kelp Gull/Black-backed Gull (*Larus dominicanus*) 1x4 (m4)
Red-billed Gull (*Larus novaehollandiae*) 1x3 (m3)
Black-billed Gull (*Larus bulleri*) 2x20 (m30)
Welcome Swallow (*Hirundo neoxena*) 1x1 (m1)

South Island Pied Oystercatcher is common throughout New Zealand. On the Firth of Thames I found it to be the easiest wader/shorebird to identify from a distance thanks to its contrasting plumage.

Site 4: Tiritiri Matangi (Auckland, New Zealand)

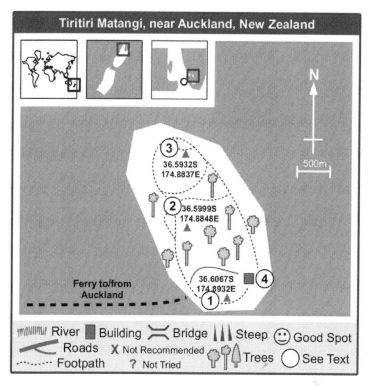

GPS coords 36.6067S 174.8932E

"An island with native forest free of non-native predators."

I saw Kokako on the **Wattle Walk** making it my favourite spot!

Spotless Crake is generally very difficult to see. Other birdwatchers have had success finding it in the wetland areas on Tiritiri Matangi island.

Here are descriptions of the points on the map (based on my visit in summer 2016):

(1) The Wattle Walk runs between the ferry and the visitor centre. It is named after wattle trees. This is where I saw Kokako.

(2) The Kaweran Bush Walk has a series of boardwalks at different levels. These offer good views through the native bush for forest birds.

(3) Silvester Wetlands is at the far north of the island.

(4) The accommodation, visitor centre and other buildings are at the top of an approximately 1km road from the ferry. Some visitors will just come to here and do some short walks. This area is good enough that you can easily see just as much as someone who goes for a longer walk all around the island.

On a 1 day visit in summer 2016 I saw 21 species of native bird:- (I also saw the non-native species House Sparrow, Blackbird, Song Thrush, Myna Bird, Goldfinch, Starling and Brown Quail.)

Little Penguin/Blue Penguin (*Eudyptula minor*) 1x1 (m1)
Variable Oystercatcher (*Haematopus unicolor*) 1x2 (m2)
Australasian Gannet (*Morus serrator*) 2x1 (m1)
Little Shag (*Phalacrocorax melanoleucos*) 3x1 (m1)
Purple Swamphen/Pukeko (*Porphyrio melanotus*) 1x2 (m2)
Kelp Gull/Black-backed Gull (*Larus dominicanus*) 5x2 (m4)
Red-billed Gull (*Larus novaehollandiae*) 3x3 (m5)
White-fronted Tern (*Sterna striata*) 1x1 (m1)
New Zealand Pigeon (*Hemiphaga novaeseelandiae*) 7x2 (m2)
Red-crowned Parakeet (*Cyanoramphus novaezelandiae*) 6x2 (m3)
Morepork (*Ninox novaeseelandiae*) 1x1 (m1)
Sacred Kingfisher (*Todiramphus sanctus*) 1x1 (m1)
North Island Kokako (*Callaeas wilsoni*) 1x1 (m1)
North Island Saddleback (*Philesturnus rufusater*) 9x3 (m11)
Stitchbird (*Notiomystis cincta*) 3x2 (m2)
Bellbird (*Anthornis melanura*) 18x2 (m2)
Tui (*Prosthemadera novaeseelandiae*) 27x2 (m7)
Whitehead (*Mohoua albicilla*) 10x2 (m2)
New Zealand Fantail (*Rhipidura fuliginosa*) 5x2 (m2)
North Island Robin (*Petroica longipes*) 1x1 (m1)
Welcome Swallow (*Hirundo neoxena*) 9x3 (m5)

As well as rarer species Tiritiri Matangi island has very large populations of the more common native birds such as this Bellbird. I was amazed by how many I saw when I visited in 2016.

Site 10: Coastal Walkway (Auckland, New Zealand)

GPS coords 36.9460S 174.7613E

"Waterbirds including New Zealand Dotterel."

I particularly enjoyed seeing New Zealand Dotterel from the **hide at position 2 on the map**.

The Coastal Walkway is a path along an industrial area to the south-west of Auckland. It starts from Ambury Regional Park http://regionalparks.aucklandcouncil.govt.nz/ambury and runs south. The full path is approximately 10km long and the site map shows the top section which I explored.

Here are descriptions of the points on the map based on my visit in summer 2016:

(1) From the visitor centre there is a short, circular walk through the fields. I saw Purple Swamphen feeding in the grass, Skylarks singing in

the sky and waders (shorebirds in American English) feeding on the mudflats.

(2) I had views of nesting New Zealand Dotterel from this hide. I also saw South Island Pied Oystercatcher on the shingle banks and groups of waders/shorebirds (mainly South Island Pied Oystercatcher, Knot and Bar-tailed Godwit) flying past over the river.

(3) There is a small lake here with more views over the river/sea. I saw Black Swans on the water. Pied Shag were perched on the rocks and feeding near the shore. Ducks, Masked Lapwing and White-faced Heron were on the lake.

On my half-day visit in summer 2016 I saw 14 species of native bird:- (I also saw the non-native species House Sparrow, Blackbird, Song Thrush, Myna Bird, Goldfinch, Starling and Brown Quail.)

Black Swan (*Cygnus atratus*) 1x30 (m30)
Paradise Shelduck (*Tadorna variegata*) 2x16 (m30)
Knot (*Calidris canutus*) 3x37 (m50)
Bar-tailed Godwit (*Limosa lapponica*) 2x5 (m5)
Variable Oystercatcher (*Haematopus unicolor*) 2x4 (m5)
South Island Pied Oystercatcher (*Haematopus finschi*) 5x8 (m15)
Pied Stilt/Black-winged Stilt (*Himantopus himantopus*) 4x6 (m15)
New Zealand Dotterel (*Charadrius obscurus*) 1x2 (m2)
Pied Shag (*Phalacrocorax varius*) 1x3 (m3)
Little Shag (*Phalacrocorax melanoleucos*) 1x1 (m1)
White-faced Heron (*Egretta novaehollandiae*) 8x8 (m25)
Purple Swamphen/Pukeko (*Porphyrio melanotus*) 6x5 (m7)
Kelp Gull/Black-backed Gull (*Larus dominicanus*) 4x2 (m3)
Welcome Swallow (*Hirundo neoxena*) 4x2 (m2)

Location 17: Whirinaki (New Zealand)

Whirinaki, New Zealand

River Road 38.6756N 176.6990E

Okahu Road

dir. Rotorua

Murupara

Minginui

Central Whirinaki

Moerangi

Skip's

Roger's

Mangamate

N

5km

38.7872N 176.6711E

Plateau Road

Hut names in italics.

38.7787N 176.6833E

River — Roads · · · Footpath — Building — Bridge — City/Town/Place — Site — Trees

"An ancient, native forest with Blue Duck and other native birds."

My favourite section of the forest was the **footpath between the River Road car park and Moerangi Hut**.

Whirinaki is pronounced "Firinaki". There are predator controls in many places, primarily positioned to protect the strong local population of Blue Duck. The Blue Duck live on the rivers and are said to be most easily seen at dawn and dusk. Other native birds also benefit from the predator controls, making this even more of a good place for birdwatchers.

This location description is based on my one week hike here in summer 2016. I think the tall native trees are spectacular and that if Whirinaki were not so far from the main tourist routes it would be a much more popular destination.

My hike in Whirinaki started at River Road car park and finished at Okahu car park. I had to make in excess of 100 river crossings and also deal with landslides and fallen trees along the trails. This is a breakdown of my route which also serves an overview of the park:

(1) **River Road Car Park** is a popular entrance to the park. Some good day walks of different lengths start here. (GPS coords 38.6756S 176.6990E)

(2) Around **Central Whirinaki Hut** I recommend looking up in the trees for parakeets and other birds. This is the highest quality hut in the area. Many people do a 2 day hike north-south or south-north between Plateau Road and River Road using this to stay in overnight. Often a group will car share and leave a vehicle at each end. (GPS coords 38.6756S 176.6990E)

(3) I turned up and away from the river at the **path junction** to continue heading towards Mangamate. (GPS coords 38.7872S 176.6711E)

(4) I then encountered a second **path junction** en route to Mangamate. (GPS coords 38.7787S 176.6833E)

(5) **Mangamate Hut** is useful to join the other huts together to form a longer route. It connects what are often described as two different parts of the forest (the eastern and western sides). (GPS coords 38.7557S 176.6891E)

(6) I continued into the eastern section of the park and stayed at the secluded **Moerangi Hut** where I got good views of forest birds. (GPS coords 38.7477S 176.7236E)

(7) You may share **Roger's Hut** with hunters who come to shoot the non-native deer. Skip's Hut is nearby and is also used by hikers, wildlife watchers and hunters. (GPS coords 38.7529S 176.7893E)

(8) There is a day walk starting at **Okahu Road Car Park** but I prefer the day walks from the River Road end. (GPS coords 38.6767S 176.8098E)

Whirinaki Forest Holidays is a local family business http://www.whirinakiforestholidays.co.nz/ (GPS coords 38.5935S 176.7712E) based to the west of the park that provides accommodation and shuttle buses between the different entry points to the park. Their flexible pick-up and drop-off service makes Whirinaki more accessible.

The forest at Whirinaki is one of the few remaining areas of ancient trees in New Zealand.

Wildlife of Whirinaki

On my 6 day hike in 2017 I saw the following 17 species of native birds:- (I also heard a lot of birds, often in the tops of trees, including Grey Warbler, but as I was hiking could not stop and look at them all. I heard the most birds in the sections with predator trapping. A local ranger reported seeing Yellow-fronted Parakeet and Shining Bronze-Cuckoo as well.) (I also saw the non-native species Blackbird, Chaffinch and Song Thrush.)

Bush Falcon/New Zealand Falcon (*Falco novaeseelandiae*) 1x1 (m1)
New Zealand Pigeon (*Hemiphaga novaeseelandiae*) 2x1 (m1)
Kaka (*Nestor meridionalis*) 10x2 (m6)
Long-tailed Cuckoo (*Eudynamys taitensis*) 1x1 (m1)
Morepork (*Ninox novaeseelandiae*) 1x1 (m1)
Sacred Kingfisher (*Todiramphus sanctus*) 1x1 (m1)
Rifleman (*Acanthisitta chloris*) 2x3 (m4)
Stitchbird (*Notiomystis cincta*) 3x2 (m2)
Grey Warbler (*Gerygone igata*) 3x2 (m2)
Bellbird (*Anthornis melanura*) 1x1 (m1)
Tui (*Prosthemadera novaeseelandiae*) 12x2 (m2)
Whitehead (*Mohoua albicilla*) 10x2 (m2)
New Zealand Fantail (*Rhipidura fuliginosa*) 8x2 (m3)
Tomtit (*Petroica macrocephala*) 6x2 (m2)
North Island Robin (*Petroica longipes*) 10x2 (m2)
Silvereye (*Zosterops lateralis*) 1x1 (m1)

Welcome Swallow (*Hirundo neoxena*) 3x2 (m2)

I saw lots of New Zealand Red Admiral in Whirinaki.

New Zealand Birds and Birdwatching

This review of New Zealand birds includes things I discovered first-hand on my visit in 2016 and also knowledge I gained from general-interest wildlife books, research papers and trip reports from other visitors. As usual I am not including references but my standard approach applies which is that I am trying to only say things which are generally accepted and can be easily confirmed in multiple books (or other media/formats). The Nature Travel Guide is intended to be an overall review of wildlife that does not get too distracted by extreme detail.

At any site in New Zealand the local bird numbers can vary drastically from year to year depending on the population of predators. Success of trapping, the amount of poison baiting and whether there has been a high fall of beech seeds (this food bonanza can boost Stoat populations) all impact on predator numbers.

In my experience the most common woodland birds are Tui, Bellbird, Grey Warbler, New Zealand Pigeon and Silvereye. Silvereye is a self-introduced species that does not need native forest to live. The native Tui seems to be adaptable and to have found ways to live even away from native trees. Bellbird is a nectar-feeder which often takes advantage of plantings of native flowers in parks and gardens. I have found that the Grey Warbler is difficult to see but can be heard regularly. New Zealand Pigeon feed on the ground and in trees, although unless introduced predators are being controlled birdwatchers report that they seem to stay off the ground.

More common non-woodland birds included Spur-winged Plover, South Island Pied Oystercatcher and Swamp Harrier. The Spur-winged Plover is a self-introduced species from Australia that feeds on grassland and also on the coast like other waders (shorebirds in American English). The South Island Pied Oystercatcher is a native wader/shorebird that, just like oystercatchers all over the world, is adaptable, found in many different habitats and is relatively common. The Swamp Harrier is a bird of prey often seen gliding over the countryside looking down for food to scavenge: It feeds mainly in open terrain, which is perhaps why it has survived the clearance of the native forest and can now be seen regularly all over New Zealand.

Some use the large number of self-introduced species to argue that nature is continually changing and that the human impacts are not so bad. I think it is more likely that the human damage to the environment is the reason that these new birds have been able to colonise. It seems likely to me that these bird species have regularly been blown over for millions of years but that they have previously found an efficient, self-contained ecosystem that did not have room for new species. Perhaps the old ecosystem has been so badly damaged that a new one is developing to take its place.

The Red-billed Gull is a common sight in New Zealand. In my experience it is more common than the similar Black-billed Gull and more adaptable to different habitats.

The Pied Shag is the most common shag I saw on my 2016 visit to New Zealand. It has white running down the head and neck in a relatively straight line. The similar Little Shag has the white on the face forming more of a circle.

I have seen White-fronted Tern all around the coast of New Zealand.

Tomtits live on the North Island and South Island. I have known them to be very inquisitive: coming up very close and then flying off after a few seconds.

Full List of Native Birds

I have counted exactly 100 species of native bird that are possible on a trip to New Zealand (I did not make it this number on purpose). This only includes seabirds that can be seen from the shore or from one of the main ferries. I have only included native birds or self-introduced birds. Any species that were introduced by humans are not included. Any species that occasionally appear in New Zealand but do not have an ongoing breeding population are not included.

Southern Brown Kiwi (*Apteryx australis*)

Okarito Brown Kiwi (*Apteryx rowi*) (Very limited range and difficult to see, although there is a paid tour operating near Franz Josef.)

Northern Brown Kiwi (*Apteryx mantelli*)

Great Spotted Kiwi (*Apteryx haastii*)

Little Spotted Kiwi (*Apteryx owenii*)

Black Swan (*Cygnus atratus*)

Paradise Shelduck (*Tadorna variegata*)

Blue Duck (*Hymenolaimus malacorhynchos*)

Grey Teal (*Anas gracilis*)

Brown Teal (*Anas chlorotis*)

Australian Shoveler (*Anas rhynchotis*)

New Zealand Scaup (*Aythya novaeseelandiae*)

Grey Duck (*Anas superciliosa*)

Great Crested Grebe/Australasian Crested Grebe (*Podiceps cristatus*)

New Zealand Dabchick (*Poliocephalus rufopectus*) (I found this difficult to see, partly as I got around by public transport and there were a limited number of wetland habitats I could visit.)

Fiordland Crested Penguin (*Eudyptes pachyrhynchus*)

Yellow-eyed Penguin (*Megadyptes antipodes*)

Little Penguin/Blue Penguin (*Eudyptula minor*)

Knot (*Calidris canutus*)

Bar-tailed Godwit (*Limosa lapponica*)

Turnstone (*Arenaria interpres*)

Variable Oystercatcher (*Haematopus unicolor*)

South Island Pied Oystercatcher (*Haematopus finschi*)

Pied Stilt/Black-winged Stilt (*Himantopus himantopus*)

Black Stilt (*Himantopus novaezelandiae*) (Very small population, possible at Mount Cook.)

Pacific Golden Plover (*Pluvialis fulva*) (A fairly rare wader/shorebird in New Zealand.)

Shore Plover (*Thinornis novaeseelandiae*) (Rare wader/shorebird that could be seen along the coast, particularly some of the islands east of Auckland.)

New Zealand Dotterel (*Charadrius obscurus*)

Banded Dotterel (*Charadrius bicinctus*)

Black-faced Dotterel (*Elseyornis melanops*) (A fairly rare wader/shorebird in New Zealand.)

Wrybill (*Anarhynchus frontalis*)

Spur-winged Plover/Masked Lapwing (*Vanellus miles*)

Northern Royal Albatross (*Diomedea sanfordi*) (Can be seen near Dunedin on the South East Coast.)

Fairy Prion (*Pachyptila turtur*) (Can be seen from the Cook Strait ferry.)

Westland Petrel (*Procellaria westlandica*) (Can be seen all around the coast. At Paparoa it is present in large numbers and is therefore easy to identify.)

Sooty Shearwater (*Puffinus griseus*)

Hutton's Shearwater/Fluttering Shearwater (*Puffinus huttoni/Puffinus gavia*)

White-faced Storm Petrel (*Pelagodroma marina*) (Difficult to see but I managed to see them feeding behind a boat on the ferry to Tiritiri Matangi Island from Auckland.)

Australasian Gannet (*Morus serrator*)

Little Black Shag (*Phalacrocorax sulcirostris*)

Pied Shag (*Phalacrocorax varius*)

Little Shag (*Phalacrocorax melanoleucos*)

Black Shag (*Phalacrocorax carbo*)

Stewart Island Shag (*Leucocarbo chalconotus*)

Spotted Shag (*Stictocarbo punctatus*)

New Zealand King Shag (*Leucocarbo carunculatus*) (Very rare but possible on the Cook Strait ferry. Can be easily seen on a birdwatching/wildlife trip from Picton.)

Great Egret/White Heron (*Ardea modesta*) (Rare but can be seen north of Franz Josef.)

Little Egret (*Egretta garzetta*) (Rare and I did not see any on my trip.)

Cattle Egret (*Ardea ibis*) (Rare and I did not see any on my trip.)

White-faced Heron (*Egretta novaehollandiae*)

Reef Heron (*Egretta sacra*) (Relatively rare with more limited range than the White-faced Heron.)

Australasian Bittern (*Botaurus poiciloptilus*) (Although this has been seen by birdwatchers in many places in New Zealand it is rare. I did not see any on my visit.)

Royal Spoonbill (*Platalea regia*)

Swamp Harrier/Australasian Harrier (*Circus approximans*)

Bush Falcon/New Zealand Falcon (*Falco novaeseelandiae*)

Banded Rail (*Gallirallus philippensis*) (Rails are difficult to see as they are secretive and spend a lot of time in thick undergrowth.)

Weka (*Gallirallus australis*)

Spotless Crake (*Porzana tabuensis*) (These are difficult to see as they are secretive and spend a lot of time in thick undergrowth.)

Baillon's Crake/Marsh Crake (*Porzana pusilla*) (Rails are difficult to see as they are secretive and spend a lot of time in thick undergrowth.)

Purple Swamphen/Pukeko (*Porphyrio melanotus*)

South Island Takake (*Porphyrio hochstetteri*) (Very rare and popular bird. Can be seen fairly reliably at many nature reserves.)

Eurasian Coot (*Fulica atra*) (A self-introduced species that I did not manage to see on my trip.)

Kelp Gull/Black-backed Gull (*Larus dominicanus*)

Red-billed Gull (*Larus novaehollandiae*)

Black-billed Gull (*Larus bulleri*)

Little Tern (*Sternula albifrons*) (On the coast in small numbers but I did not see one.)

Fairy Tern (*Sternula nereis*) (Very rare in New Zealand and you will be lucky to see one.)

Caspian Tern (*Hydroprogne caspia*)

Black-fronted Tern (*Chlidonias albostriatus*) (Locally-common east of the Southern Alps, for example at Mount Cook.)

White-fronted Tern (*Sterna striata*)

New Zealand Pigeon (*Hemiphaga novaeseelandiae*)

Kaka (*Nestor meridionalis*)

Kea (*Nestor notabilis*)

Yellow-crowned Parakeet (*Cyanoramphus auriceps*)

Orange-fronted Parakeet (*Cyanoramphus malherbi*)

Red-crowned Parakeet (*Cyanoramphus novaezelandiae*)

Shining Bronze-cuckoo (*Chrysococcyx lucidus*)

Long-tailed Cuckoo (*Eudynamys taitensis*)

Morepork (*Ninox novaeseelandiae*) (Nocturnal so very difficult to see but relatively easy to hear.)

Sacred Kingfisher (*Todiramphus sanctus*)

Rifleman (*Acanthisitta chloris*)

Rock Wren (*Xenicus gilviventris*)

North Island Kokako (*Callaeas wilsoni*)

North Island Saddleback (*Philesturnus rufusater*)

South Island Saddleback (*Philesturnus carunculatus*)

Stitchbird (*Notiomystis cincta*)

Grey Warbler (*Gerygone igata*)

Bellbird (*Anthornis melanura*)

Tui (*Prosthemadera novaeseelandiae*)

Whitehead (*Mohoua albicilla*)

Yellowhead (*Mohoua ochrocephala*)

Brown Creeper (*Mohoua novaeseelandiae*)

New Zealand Fantail (*Rhipidura fuliginosa*)

Tomtit (*Petroica macrocephala*)

North Island Robin (*Petroica longipes*)

South Island Robin (*Petroica australis*)

Fernbird (*Bowdleria punctata*) (A wetland bird that I was lucky enough to see once on my trip. Generally difficult to see.)

Silvereye (*Zosterops lateralis*)

Welcome Swallow (*Hirundo neoxena*)

New Zealand Pipit (*Anthus novaeseelandiae*) (I saw New Zealand Pipit in a few places but it was generally very rare.)

Bird Identification Notes

These notes are observations I made about how I eliminated similar species and confirmed the identifications of the birds I saw on my visit to New Zealand in 2016.

Masked Lapwing/Spur-winged Plover is a self-introduced wader/shorebird seen all over New Zealand. They can be aggressive, using the spurs in their wings to attack other birds.

New Zealand Falcon can be difficult to see without local knowledge. One of the more reliable places is Mount Cook.

Southern Brown Kiwi (*Apteryx australis*): Seen on Stewart Island so had to be this species. Also, the streaking (not spotting) was very clear. The plumage different from a Weka and the bill was seen confirming it was not a Weka.

Great Spotted Kiwi (*Apteryx haastii*): (1) When I first saw this it kept its head down the whole time and I only saw the body. I was reliant on the plumage being very different from the Weka to be sure. (2) The second time I saw the beak which confirmed my identification. I also realised that in the poor light of night-time the plumage was very difficult to see properly which I imagine might be an evolved camouflage.

Black Swan (*Cygnus atratus*): A large black bird in the water with a much longer neck than the shags or other waterbirds.

Paradise Shelduck (*Tadorna variegata*): I found the distinctive plumage of the female easy to identify. Later I realised how clear the white in the wing is, making it easy to identify in flight.

Grey Teal (*Anas gracilis*): Pale side to head, slightly different shape of body and lack of other distinguishing features.

Brown Teal (*Anas chlorotis*): I mainly identified Brown Teal from the fact it did not have any of the identifying features of the other species. It was also, obviously, very brown.

Australian Shoveler (*Anas rhynchotis*): Bill obviously large and flat with the brightly coloured male making identification easy.

New Zealand Scaup (*Aythya novaeseelandiae*): I initially saw many scaup that I was not sure were definitely New Zealand Scaup. The smaller size, scruffy tail, rich colours and diving behaviour eventually made me confident I had seen this species. Close views on some of the lakes on North Island were useful. Australian White-eyed Duck is similar.

Grey Duck (*Anas superciliosa*): This often hybridises with Mallard. I saw two birds at Milford Sound and they showed very clear facial markings with no obvious features inherited from a Mallard. Also, Milford Sound is one of the places where pure Grey Duck is said to still be found which helped me to be more confident.

Great Crested Grebe/Australasian Crested Grebe (*Podiceps cristatus*): More grey and with some red with a profile different from a shag.

Fiordland Crested Penguin (*Eudyptes pachyrhynchus*): The yellow across the top of the eye was more horizontal than for the Yellow-eyed Penguin. Also, seen in the correct place for this species.

Yellow-eyed Penguin (*Megadyptes antipodes*): Even without seeing the yellow on the head (they were a distance away), the size, overall colouring and the fact they were seen outside the typical range of Fiordland Crested Penguin made me confident they were Yellow-eyed Penguin. Later I saw the yellow on the face in the correct pattern as well.

Little Penguin/Blue Penguin (*Eudyptula minor*): Very small without the distinguishing features of the other penguins.

Knot (*Calidris canutus*): Seen in large groups so has to be one of the more common waders/shorebirds. Too small for a godwit and lacks any obvious plumage markings for other species.

Bar-tailed Godwit (*Limosa lapponica*): Large wader/shorebird with long bill. Common in New Zealand so seen in large groups whereas similar species are not very common.

Variable Oystercatcher (*Haematopus unicolor*): Typically all black. It can't be anything else.

South Island Pied Oystercatcher (*Haematopus finschi*): There was white on the underside which clearly went up right next to the wing.

Pied Stilt/Black-winged Stilt (*Himantopus himantopus*): The first bird I saw had muddy plumage but the long legs and white-and-black plumage were obvious even if the mud made it indistinct.

Black Stilt (*Himantopus novaezelandiae*): I initially thought it might be a Black-winged Stilt with unusually dark plumage. It is generally black with white dappling.

Pacific Golden Plover (*Pluvialis fulva*): Plovers have short, thicker bills whereas other waders/shorebirds generally have longer bills or if the bills are short they are more slim. Dotterels also have short bills but they are whiter with lines in the plumage whereas Knot are all-over grey.

New Zealand Dotterel (*Charadrius obscurus*): This took me a while to identify. The general look was of a dotterel (pale with a short bill). The lack of any lines in the plumage across the front meant it was New Zealand Dotterel.

Banded Dotterel (*Charadrius bicinctus*): The two lines across the front of the bird looked just right.

Wrybill (*Anarhynchus frontalis*): The bill was obviously curved when it looked straight at me so it had to be Wrybill. Before I saw the bill from the front it looked like a plover or dotterel with a single band across the throat and grey plumage.

Spur-winged Plover/Masked Lapwing (*Vanellus miles*): The yellow on the face was distinctive.

White-capped Albatross/Shy Albatross (*Thalassarche cauta*): Seen repeatedly from the boat to Stewart Island. I got a good photograph and the combination of facial markings and the colours on the upper and lower wings made me confident it was this species. Generally I do not try to identify the albatrosses but with such a clear photograph, and because it was such a memorable bird during the crossing, I made an extra effort.

Northern Royal Albatross (*Diomedea sanfordi*): Seen at the colony near Dunedin so identified as this species.

Fairy Prion (*Pachyptila turtur*): The lack of dark under the head meant it was not Hutton's Shearwater/Fluttering Shearwater. The lack of dark above the wings eliminated most other seabirds. The distinctive dark line above each wing and the dark line on the face could be seen.

Westland Petrel (*Procellaria westlandica*): Seen flying onshore to the Westland Petrel colony near Punakaiki. So, mainly identified by where they were seen. Also all black and the wings looked long and thin and when flying they would often glide near the water.

Sooty Shearwater (*Puffinus griseus*): The paler underwing combined with generally dark plumage along with being fairly common made me confident it was Sooty Shearwater.

Hutton's Shearwater/Fluttering Shearwater (*Puffinus huttoni/Puffinus gavia*): As with other birdwatchers I did not try to identify which of these two common species I was seeing. The smaller size compared to the petrels and gulls, the fast wing beats, the strong change from dark to light plumage on the throat and the pale underwing were used to make the identification.

White-faced Storm Petrel (*Pelagodroma marina*): Seen behind a boat off the shore of Auckland repeatedly diving gently down to the surface of the water. They looked almost butterfly-like. The colours on the side of the head looked exactly correct.

Australasian Gannet (*Morus serrator*): Larger, heavier and with more-pointed wings than other birds flying over the sea.

Little Black Shag (*Phalacrocorax sulcirostris*): Only seen on the North Island. Small size, all black with pale bill.

Pied Shag (*Phalacrocorax varius*): Unlike on Little Shag, the white continued all the way down the front. The white was not limited to the face.

Little Shag (*Phalacrocorax melanoleucos*): I found the Little Pied Shag and Pied Shag could look very similar. I used the more rounded shape of the head, including the white line in the plumage being curved, to identify Little Pied Shag.

Black Shag (*Phalacrocorax carbo*): All dark and much larger than the other shags.

Stewart Island Shag (*Leucocarbo chalconotus*): Unlike the Pied Shag the white underneath does not extend all the way up to the eye. And for the darker forms, the bird was all black and lacked the paler section around the face of the Black Shag.

Spotted Shag (*Stictocarbo punctatus*): The line running down each side of the neck made me confident it was not another species of shag.

New Zealand King Shag (*Leucocarbo carunculatus*): Seen at a known breeding colony from the Cook Strait ferry. Although they were a long way away the size could be seen by comparison with nearby gulls and the amount of white in the plumage could also be seen.

White-faced Heron (*Egretta novaehollandiae*): The white circle around the eye was very clear. I also found the pale-grey plumage useful to be sure.

Reef Heron (*Egretta sacra*): Clearly all dark. Seen in the Golden Bay area so in the correct place.

Royal Spoonbill (*Platalea regia*): The only spoonbill likely in New Zealand. The large, heavy bill is very distinctive once seen from a good angle.

Swamp Harrier/Australasian Harrier (*Circus approximans*): This is the only large raptor likely to be seen so I found it easy to identify. Once I had seen a few, the distinctive soaring flight became easy to recognise.

Bush Falcon/New Zealand Falcon (*Falco novaeseelandiae*): I thought the New Zealand Falcon was much darker and compact than a Swamp Harrier. The shorter, more-pointed wings flapped much faster than a harrier's.

Weka (*Gallirallus australis*): Compared to a kiwi it has a very clear line above the eye and a much shorter bill. The tail is often raised but not always. Obviously a kiwi is very unlikely but I found it useful to get familiar with the Weka so I would be well prepared for identifying kiwis on my nocturnal forest walks.

Purple Swamphen/Pukeko (*Porphyrio melanotus*): When I visited this was the only bluish bird of this size with a red bill to be seen commonly on the mainland.

South Island Takake (*Porphyrio hochstetteri*): The bill really is very big. It also looks to me like it has a thicker neck and generally less slim profile.

Kelp Gull/Black-backed Gull (*Larus dominicanus*): Much larger than the other gulls. Also has very clear dark tops to the wings.

Red-billed Gull (*Larus novaehollandiae*): Red bill and lots of white on the end of the wing.

Black-billed Gull (*Larus bulleri*): Black bill and not very much white on the end of the wing.

Fairy Tern (*Sternula nereis*): Red bill with white on the forehead. A small tern seen along a section of coast where they are known to breed in small numbers.

Caspian Tern (*Hydroprogne caspia*): Compared to other possible terns the bill is very large.

Black-fronted Tern (*Chlidonias albostriatus*): Because of the similarity in name I thought it would look similar to a White-fronted Tern. I felt it looked very different with grey in the plumage and a short yellow/orange bill. The complete black cap and the bill were distinctive.

White-fronted Tern (*Sterna striata*): Seen in the summer. Had a black cap, a black bill and a white forehead. This distinguished it from the Black-fronted Tern.

New Zealand Pigeon (*Hemiphaga novaeseelandiae*): I felt the shape was distinctive compared to other pigeons. Also, the clear dark green on the head becoming white further down made a pattern that was visible even from a distance.

Kaka (*Nestor meridionalis*): I had clear views so was certain they were all brown without the extra colours of the Kea.

Kea (*Nestor notabilis*): The colour under the wing was seen as it flew past meaning it could not be the all-brown Kaka.

Yellow-crowned Parakeet (*Cyanoramphus auriceps*): Extensive yellow seen on the top of the head. One was seen with only a small amount of yellow which meant it may have been a hybrid with the Red-crowned Parakeet.

Red-crowned Parakeet (*Cyanoramphus novaezelandiae*): (1) Only red on the top of the head and no other colours. (2) I started seeing more of these once I learnt to look up if I heard the quiet noise of scraps falling from the tops of trees as they were feeding.

Shining Bronze-cuckoo (*Chrysococcyx lucidus*): Cuckoo-shaped with metallic green on its back.

Long-tailed Cuckoo (*Eudynamys taitensis*): Brown, long tail with a fork. White line above the eye.

Morepork (*Ninox novaeseelandiae*): The only other possible owl is the introduced Little Owl and this did not look anything like a Little Owl.

Sacred Kingfisher (*Todiramphus sanctus*): (1) The only likely kingfisher in New Zealand. Seen from a distance the bright metallic colours were not obvious but the long, thick bill and body shape were distinctive. Also it was seen perching near water and diving straight into the water from the perch. (2) Often seen in tops of trees calling a bit like a New Zealand Falcon.

Rifleman (*Acanthisitta chloris*): Once I realised the males were greenish yellow and the females mainly a streaked brown these were much easier. I kept forgetting to use the short tail to make identification really easy!

North Island Kokako (*Callaeas wilsoni*): Distinctive plumage. I found the blue a bit difficult to see but the shape of the pale area around the face was in exactly the correct shape.

North Island Saddleback (*Philesturnus rufusater*): Distinctive and seen on North Island. Sometimes I would confuse it with Blackbird, but the Blackbird lacks the red on the back.

South Island Saddleback (*Philesturnus carunculatus*): Plumage colours distinctive and seen on Ulva Island so could not be the North Island species.

Stitchbird (*Notiomystis cincta*): The male has very obvious plumage and is larger than a lot of the other song birds. The female is smaller and I often confused it with female Bellbird although the Stitchbird is less green.

Grey Warbler (*Gerygone igata*): (1) A distinctive call that I started using to make identification easier. Initially I used the overall plainness and lack of other features to identify them. (2) Later I realised that the white line on the end of the tail was useful in identification with the only similar bird also having white at the end of the tail being Rifleman which is much smaller and darker. (3) Later I also learnt to identify Grey Warbler from the fact it lacks any distinguishing features. So, if it was not obviously any other bird then it was a Grey Warbler. (4) The female is much smaller than the male and I learnt to identify the female just from the small, slim shape.

Bellbird (*Anthornis melanura*): To me this looks green with a yellow line below the wing: a distinctive plumage pattern.

Tui (*Prosthemadera novaeseelandiae*): Compared to a Blackbird (an introduced species) I thought the wings and tail had more pointed corners. Also, the Tui has a white front edge to the wing when flying. I often found the white below the throat difficult to see but if I did see it then obviously it made identification easy. The call varies locally.

Whitehead (*Mohoua albicilla*): In poor light can look grey but then the shape is distinctive. Once the white head has been seen it is obvious. In forest it seems to be mainly higher in the trees but in open areas can be low down in bushes.

Yellowhead (*Mohoua ochrocephala*): I was surprised just how yellow it was. Could not be anything else.

Brown Creeper (*Mohoua novaeseelandiae*): I almost always saw the grey head very clearly. This would confuse me as I kept forgetting that the head was not brown! Once I started remembering, this identification was easy.

New Zealand Fantail (*Rhipidura fuliginosa*): Very distinctive.

Tomtit (*Petroica macrocephala*): In the panic of identification I initially confused this with a robin. Once I learnt that the Tomtit has a small spot of white above the bill and much darker black plumage it was easy.

North Island Robin (*Petroica longipes*): Has slightly less white on the belly than the South Island Robin but is found on a different island so easy to identify. Also see Tomtit comments.

South Island Robin (*Petroica australis*): See Tomtit comments.

Fernbird (*Bowdleria punctata*): When I first saw this I was stumped. I think a good name would be "Brown Streaked Bird With Clear Eye Stripe". The fern-like tail was useful but often hidden from sight.

Silvereye (*Zosterops lateralis*): Very distinctive.

Welcome Swallow (*Hirundo neoxena*): Nothing else like it here so I found this easy to identify.

New Zealand Pipit (*Anthus novaeseelandiae*): To me it was clearly different from a Skylark in terms of body shape and the pattern of brown on the sides. Also, the pale line above the eye was very large and obvious. It was seen perching on bushes and posts and generally behaving differently to the introduced Skylark.

Birdwatching Itineraries for New Zealand

For birdwatchers I recommend visiting in the New Zealand summer. All the breeding birds will be active and are joined by the migrating waders (shorebirds in American English) that are avoiding the winter in the northern hemisphere.

If you visit in October/November the Westland Petrel can still be seen at their breeding grounds (at the Paparoa location). If you visit later in the summer then the Westland Petrel will have dispersed offshore all around the coast, for example at Kaikoura.

This is a Spotted Shag on its nest at Oamaru on the south-east coast of South Island.

Single-Location Itineraries

My personal favourite place to stay for a week or more would be Stewart Island. It is a beautiful island with many different day hikes and longer hikes, pelagic cruises and Ulva Island to visit.

If you like hiking and enjoy camping or staying in huts then I recommend trying a multi-day hike at Whirinaki or Kahurangi.

Auckland would be a good base if you want to be able to enjoy a variety of day trips to see different wildlife and also have non-wildlife, city-type activities to do.

Brown Teal is one of many New Zealand birds with a limited range. They are easy to see but only if you go to certain places such as Zealandia (near Wellington) or Tawharanui Open Sanctuary (near Auckland).

Quick Itinerary (whole country, 1-2 weeks)

I think a quick birdwatching stay in New Zealand is more difficult than in other countries. Some of the top destinations used by tour companies and self-guided visitors are Ulva Island (Stewart Island), Marlborough Sounds, Kapiti Island (near Wellington), the Firth of Thames (near Auckland) and Tiritiri Matangi Island (near Auckland). These take a long time to drive between with easily 24 hours driving to get from Auckland in the north to Stewart Island in the south. The professional tour companies choose places to visit between these which breaks up the driving.

If you intend to try visiting the whole country in only a couple of weeks I think you probably have to hire a car or a campervan. You could choose some key places to visit and then add some supplementary ones to break up your driving.

Quick Itinerary (central focus, 1-2 weeks)

One quick itinerary with much less travelling would be to stay at Wellington overnight for at least one night. You can visit Kapiti Island

and Zealandia from Wellington. This gives North Island species. Then catch the ferry to Picton (Marlborough Sounds) where there are island nature reserves to add South Island species. Picton is also an excellent base for seabirds and other coastal wildlife on boat trips.

I think this central itinerary is an excellent option. You will still be able to see a lot and you can take your time more. If it were me though, I would still be tempted to do the itinerary with more driving as I would really want to visit the fantastic Stewart Island and Tiritiri Matangi Island.

On the central itinerary I think you will be mainly missing out on waders/shorebirds, some bird species that are not found in the central area and spectacles such as Mount Cook, the northern forests and Stewart Island.

I photographed this New Zealand Pigeon at Kahurangi National Park.

Backpackers or Slow Travel Itinerary (50 days)

My suggested backpacker route around New Zealand is based on the route I took and adapted slightly based on what I discovered along the way. There are a number of bus services; I chose to mainly use the Intercity http://www.intercity.co.nz/ and used advance purchase tickets to end up with a very low overall cost: they were cheap even compared to the budget/rover tickets that are available with other companies. If you are taking the bus you are not necessarily going to have access to a vehicle (although often you can inspire other people at the hostel that do have a car to join you for the day) and so in the location descriptions I include wildlife-watching options if you do not have a vehicle.

Arrive at Christchurch (or another place on the South Island).

Bus to Punakaiki, stay at Paparoa for 5 nights.

Bus to Franz Josef, stay at Franz Josef for 3 nights.

Bus to Haast, stay at Haast for 2 nights. (This is a difficult place to explore without your own transport. However, you can visit Munro Beach if you are OK with hitching back to Haast.)

Bus to Te Anau, stay for 3 nights.

Bus to Milford Sound, stay for 2 nights.

Bus to Invercargill, stay for 2 nights. (Site in the South East Coast location.)

Ferry to Stewart Island, stay for 11 nights.

Bus to Dunedin, stay for 2 nights. (Site in the South East Coast location.)

Bus to Oamaru, stay for 2 nights. (Site in the South East Coast location.)

Bus to Cromwell, stay 1 night. (This is only because you cannot get to Mount Cook in 1 day by public transport although that might change or I may have missed an option.)

Bus to Mount Cook, stay for 3 nights. (You could split the bus from Cromwell to Mount Cook at Twizel and stay there to look for waterbirds on the lakes.)

Bus to Christchurch, stay 1 night. (Because I could not find a way to Kaikoura in 1 day.)

Bus to Kaikoura, stay 3 nights.

Bus to Picton, stay 1 night. (Stay overnight at Picton to be ready for the first ferry of the day when the wildlife watching is generally better than later crossings. You might stay longer, see the Marlborough Sounds location overview for some suggestions.)

Ferry from Picton to Wellington across Cook Strait, stay at Wellington for 4 nights.

Bus to Auckland, stay at Auckland for 4 nights.

If you have flown to New Zealand you can try to fly out of New Zealand from Auckland to save returning to the start.

I saw a total of 77 species when I tried the backpackers itinerary during October to November 2016:

Southern Brown Kiwi (*Apteryx australis*) (seen at Stewart Island)
Great Spotted Kiwi (*Apteryx haastii*) (seen at Paparoa)

Black Swan (*Cygnus atratus*) (seen at 5 locations:- Haast, Stewart Island, South East Coast, Mount Cook, Auckland)

Paradise Shelduck (*Tadorna variegata*) (seen at 8 locations:- Paparoa, Haast, Fiordland, Stewart Island, South East Coast, Mount Cook, Wellington, Auckland)

Grey Teal (*Anas gracilis*) (seen at 2 locations:- South East Coast, Wellington)

Brown Teal (*Anas chlorotis*) (seen at Wellington)

Australian Shoveler (*Anas rhynchotis*) (seen at South East Coast)

New Zealand Scaup (*Aythya novaeseelandiae*) (seen at Wellington)

Grey Duck (*Anas superciliosa*) (seen at Fiordland)

Great Crested Grebe/Australasian Crested Grebe (*Podiceps cristatus*) (seen at Fiordland)

Fiordland Crested Penguin (*Eudyptes pachyrhynchus*) (seen at Haast)

Yellow-eyed Penguin (*Megadyptes antipodes*) (seen at South East Coast)

Little Penguin/Blue Penguin (*Eudyptula minor*) (seen at 3 locations:- Stewart Island, South East Coast, Auckland)

Knot (*Calidris canutus*) (seen at Auckland)

Bar-tailed Godwit (*Limosa lapponica*) (seen at Auckland)

Variable Oystercatcher (*Haematopus unicolor*) (seen at 7 locations:- Paparoa, Haast, Fiordland, Stewart Island, South East Coast, Wellington, Auckland)

South Island Pied Oystercatcher (*Haematopus finschi*) (seen at 7 locations:- Paparoa, Haast, Fiordland, Stewart Island, South East Coast, Mount Cook, Auckland)

Pied Stilt/Black-winged Stilt (*Himantopus himantopus*) (seen at 2 locations:- South East Coast, Auckland)

Black Stilt (*Himantopus novaezelandiae*) (seen at Mount Cook)

New Zealand Dotterel (*Charadrius obscurus*) (seen at Auckland)

Banded Dotterel (*Charadrius bicinctus*) (seen at 3 locations:- Paparoa, Stewart Island, Mount Cook)

Wrybill (*Anarhynchus frontalis*) (seen at Mount Cook)

Spur-winged Plover/Masked Lapwing (*Vanellus miles*) (seen at 5 locations:- Haast, Fiordland, South East Coast, Mount Cook, Auckland)

White-capped Albatross/Shy Albatross (*Thalassarche cauta*) (seen at 2 locations:- spare, Stewart Island)

Northern Royal Albatross (*Diomedea sanfordi*) (seen at South East Coast)

Fairy Prion (*Pachyptila turtur*) (seen at Cook Strait)

Westland Petrel (*Procellaria westlandica*) (seen at Paparoa)

Sooty Shearwater (*Puffinus griseus*) (seen at 2 locations:- spare, Stewart Island)

Hutton's Shearwater/Fluttering Shearwater (*Puffinus huttoni/Puffinus gavia*) (seen at 2 locations:- Stewart Island, South East Coast)

White-faced Storm Petrel (*Pelagodroma marina*) (seen at Auckland)

Australasian Gannet (*Morus serrator*) (seen at 5 locations:- Haast, South East Coast, Cook Strait, Wellington, Auckland)

Little Black Shag (*Phalacrocorax sulcirostris*) (seen at Wellington)

Pied Shag (*Phalacrocorax varius*) (seen at 4 locations:- Stewart Island, Cook Strait, Wellington, Auckland)

Little Shag (*Phalacrocorax melanoleucos*) (seen at 7 locations:- Paparoa, Haast, Fiordland, Stewart Island, South East Coast, Wellington, Auckland)

Black Shag (*Phalacrocorax carbo*) (seen at 4 locations:- Haast, Fiordland, Stewart Island, South East Coast)

Stewart Island Shag (*Leucocarbo chalconotus*) (seen at 2 locations:- Stewart Island, South East Coast)

Spotted Shag (*Stictocarbo punctatus*) (seen at 4 locations:- spare, Stewart Island, South East Coast, Cook Strait)

New Zealand King Shag (*Leucocarbo carunculatus*) (seen at Cook Strait)

White-faced Heron (*Egretta novaehollandiae*) (seen at 5 locations:- Paparoa, Stewart Island, South East Coast, Mount Cook, Auckland)

Royal Spoonbill (*Platalea regia*) (seen at South East Coast)

Swamp Harrier/Australasian Harrier (*Circus approximans*) (seen at 6 locations:- Paparoa, Haast, Fiordland, Stewart Island, South East Coast, Mount Cook)

Bush Falcon/New Zealand Falcon (*Falco novaeseelandiae*) (seen at Mount Cook)

Weka (*Gallirallus australis*) (seen at 4 locations:- Paparoa, Fiordland, Stewart Island, Wellington)

Purple Swamphen/Pukeko (*Porphyrio melanotus*) (seen at 4 locations:- Paparoa, Haast, Mount Cook, Auckland)

South Island Takake (*Porphyrio hochstetteri*) (seen at Wellington)

Kelp Gull/Black-backed Gull (*Larus dominicanus*) (seen at 10 locations:- Paparoa, Haast, spare, Fiordland, Stewart Island, South East Coast, Mount Cook, Cook Strait, Wellington, Auckland)

Red-billed Gull (*Larus novaehollandiae*) (seen at 7 locations:- Paparoa, Haast, Stewart Island, South East Coast, Cook Strait, Wellington, Auckland)

Black-billed Gull (*Larus bulleri*) (seen at Fiordland)

Caspian Tern (*Hydroprogne caspia*) (seen at 2 locations:- Haast, Auckland)

Black-fronted Tern (*Chlidonias albostriatus*) (seen at Mount Cook)

White-fronted Tern (*Sterna striata*) (seen at 6 locations:- Paparoa, Haast, Stewart Island, South East Coast, Cook Strait, Auckland)

New Zealand Pigeon (*Hemiphaga novaeseelandiae*) (seen at 7 locations:- Paparoa, Haast, Fiordland, Stewart Island, South East Coast, Wellington, Auckland)

Kaka (*Nestor meridionalis*) (seen at 2 locations:- Stewart Island, Wellington)

Kea (*Nestor notabilis*) (seen at 3 locations:- Haast, Fiordland, Mount Cook)

Yellow-crowned Parakeet (*Cyanoramphus auriceps*) (seen at Stewart Island)

Red-crowned Parakeet (*Cyanoramphus novaezelandiae*) (seen at 3 locations:- Stewart Island, Wellington, Auckland)

Shining Bronze-cuckoo (*Chrysococcyx lucidus*) (seen at Haast)

Morepork (*Ninox novaeseelandiae*) (seen at Auckland)

Sacred Kingfisher (*Todiramphus sanctus*) (seen at 3 locations:- Stewart Island, South East Coast, Auckland)

Rifleman (*Acanthisitta chloris*) (seen at Mount Cook)

North Island Kokako (*Callaeas wilsoni*) (seen at Auckland)

North Island Saddleback (*Philesturnus rufusater*) (seen at 2 locations:- Wellington, Auckland)

South Island Saddleback (*Philesturnus carunculatus*) (seen at Stewart Island)

Stitchbird (*Notiomystis cincta*) (seen at 2 locations:- Wellington, Auckland)

Grey Warbler (*Gerygone igata*) (seen at 5 locations:- Paparoa, Fiordland, Stewart Island, Mount Cook, Wellington)

Bellbird (*Anthornis melanura*) (seen at 7 locations:- Paparoa, Haast, Fiordland, Stewart Island, Mount Cook, Wellington, Auckland)

Tui (*Prosthemadera novaeseelandiae*) (seen at 7 locations:- Paparoa, Haast, Fiordland, Stewart Island, South East Coast, Wellington, Auckland)

Whitehead (*Mohoua albicilla*) (seen at 2 locations:- Wellington, Auckland)

Yellowhead (*Mohoua ochrocephala*) (seen at Stewart Island)

Brown Creeper (*Mohoua novaeseelandiae*) (seen at 3 locations:- Haast, Fiordland, Stewart Island)

New Zealand Fantail (*Rhipidura fuliginosa*) (seen at 7 locations:- Paparoa, Haast, Fiordland, Stewart Island, Mount Cook, Wellington, Auckland)

Tomtit (*Petroica macrocephala*) (seen at 5 locations:- Paparoa, Haast, Fiordland, Stewart Island, Mount Cook)

North Island Robin (*Petroica longipes*) (seen at 2 locations:- Wellington, Auckland)

South Island Robin (*Petroica australis*) (seen at 3 locations:- Paparoa, Fiordland, Stewart Island)

Silvereye (*Zosterops lateralis*) (seen at 6 locations:- Paparoa, Haast, Fiordland, Stewart Island, South East Coast, Mount Cook)

Welcome Swallow (*Hirundo neoxena*) (seen at 8 locations:- Paparoa, Haast, spare, Fiordland, Stewart Island, South East Coast, Mount Cook, Auckland)

New Zealand Pipit (*Anthus novaeseelandiae*) (seen at 3 locations:- Stewart Island, Mount Cook, Wellington)

Activities

Wildlife-watching activities can add an extra dimension to a vacation, walk, cycle tour, driving stop or picnic. Alternatively you can simply read these activities as wildlife-watching articles.

Read on to find the following activities:

New Zealand Introduced Bird Bingo

New Zealand Native Bird Bingo

Mount Cook Explorer

Kiwi Tracking

Australasian Seawatching

New Zealand Introduced Bird Bingo (Activity)

These are some of my favourite introduced bird species in New Zealand. Which do you like? Which can you see? (They may not all be possible, depending on where you are and the time of year.)

Do you want to give yourself a score? Score either 1 point for three in a row (horizontal or vertical); 2 points for three in a row (diagonal); 3 points for a vertical cross (+); 4 points for a diagonal cross (X) or; 5 points for all nine.

(1) Masked Lapwing (self-introduced from Australia). This is a distinctive bird with a yellow mask. Also called Spur-winged Plover because it has a spur on each wing that can be used to attack other birds.

(2) Chaffinch (from Europe). This is a widespread bird in Europe where it lives in many habitats. It has been similarly successful since it was introduced to New Zealand. It is the only bird you will see which is red and shaped like this. The female is brown.

(3) Silvereye (self-introduced from Australia). The Silvereye appeared in New Zealand after probably being blown over from Australia (another possibility is stowing away on a ship or being released from captivity). Maybe it was a pregnant female that made the crossing or a group of Silvereye that crossed together: there had to be at least one male and one female to be able to breed.

(4) Starling (from Europe). The Starling was also introduced to North America where it has also been very successful. A small, dark bird with tiny white spots and some bright greens and blues in the plumage.

(5) Yellowhammer (from Europe). The Yellowhammer is often perched on bushes in open habitat. It was introduced from Europe although it is now common in parts of New Zealand and many people think of it as native. This is the only bird with such a bright yellow head.

(6) Blackbird (from Europe). The Blackbird is larger than a Starling with a thicker, orange bill.

(7) Australasian Magpie (introduced from Australia to help keep farmland free of pest insects). The magpie is a distinctive black-and-white bird.

(8) Myna Bird (introduced from Asia). The plumage is mainly brown with white in the wing. The orange bill and eye area are visible from close up. The myna is a well-known mimic able to copy other bird's calls.

(9) Song Thrush (introduced from Europe). In Europe I often see Song Thrush eating snails. Here in New Zealand I mainly see them eating worms. Very similar in size to a Blackbird but brown with spots underneath.

New Zealand Native Bird Bingo (Activity)

These are some of my favourite native bird species of New Zealand. Which do you like? Which can you see? (They may not all be possible, depending on where you are and the time of year.)

Do you want to give yourself a score? Score either 1 point for three in a row (horizontal or vertical); 2 points for three in a row (diagonal); 3 points for a vertical cross (+); 4 points for a diagonal cross (X) or; 5 points for all nine.

(1) Paradise Shelduck. The female has a white head and brown body. The male is all dark. Look out for the ducklings in spring and early summer.

(2) Tomtit. This inquisitive bird is one of my favourites in New Zealand. It is similar to some other birds but look for the white spot above the beak. The clear line between the dark throat and white belly also help with identification.

(3) Banded Plover. I saw this all along the coast of North and South Island. Other plovers live in New Zealand but only Banded Plover have a small black band above a wide red band.

(4) Bellbird. The Bellbird is common in native bush and is also adaptable enough to be able to live in human habitats. It is green with a slightly curved bill and grey on the head.

(5) Grey Warbler. I heard the call of the Grey Warbler all over New Zealand. However, it can be difficult to see, which is why it is in the middle of the bingo grid! The female is much smaller than the male so they can look like different species. It is the only New Zealand bird that is small, grey and has a long tail.

(6) White-faced Heron. This tall bird can be seen on the coast and in wetland habitats. It has a grey body with white on the side of the face and a black bill. Challenge: can you see it catch a fish?

(7) Tui. The Tui has slightly different colours in different parts of New Zealand but is always mainly green/blue/black with the white feathers just under the bill. This native bird has adapted to many different habitats since the arrival of humans.

(8) Black Swan. Look out on rivers, lakes and in other wetland habitats.

(9) Pied Shag. The black on the top of the head and back of the neck is very clear. The white on the throat and front of the neck makes a very straight line. The Little Pied Shag is similar but smaller, with a less straight line on the side of a more rounded face.

Mount Cook Explorer (Activity)

These are some of my favourite plants, animals and behaviours to discover whilst exploring Mount Cook on South Island, New Zealand. Which do you like? Which can you see? (They may not all be possible, depending on where you are and the time of year.)

(1) Mount Cook Lily. This is actually a species of buttercup. Buttercup are an ancient flower family that has survived despite the evolution of much more sophisticated flower designs. Their internal chemistry is advanced and a possible reason they survived while other ancient flower families did not.

(2) Mountain Flax. This tough species of flax can live through the harsh winters in the mountains.

(3) Canterbury Alpine Boulder Copper. This small butterfly is common on Mount Cook in the summer.

(4) Grey Warbler. The Grey Warbler is a native species and lives mainly in the bush around the village. The female is much smaller than the male and is easily confused for a different species.

(5) Silvereye. Silvereye live in the bush and also in more open habitats. I mainly saw them on the sides of the footpaths in the scrub. The Silvereye self-introduced in approximately the early 20th century and has spread throughout New Zealand. Also look out for Yellowhammer which is an introduced species of bird from Europe that has a bright yellow head.

(6) Rifleman. The very short tail helps identify this small, insect-eating bird. It is a native New Zealand bird that is generally difficult to see. I found it easier to see at Mount Cook and others have reported the same.

(7) Black-fronted Tern. This rare, native bird is common in the braided rivers around Mount Cook. They mainly feed over the river but sometimes feed over the grassland, even coming right up to the village.

(8) New Zealand Falcon. This native bird, in the early 21st century, is breeding in the Mount Cook area. It is a powerful flyer with more pointed wings and a smaller, stockier body than the Swamp Harrier.

Kiwi Tracking (Activity)

Kiwis are only found in New Zealand.

Here are some kiwi field signs that they leave as evidence of their night-time adventures. If you can find an area with one or more of these then you might return at dusk to try to see a kiwi. If you stay quiet and stand still they may come close. Do not try to follow a kiwi as it can stress them. Avoid shining a light in their eyes as they have very good eyesight to move around at night and it can damage their eyes. Either switch off your torch or slightly cover it and turn it away from the kiwi. A red-light torch is better because scientists report that kiwis are not sensitive to it. Also, if you find a burrow you might take a closer look in the day (never poke anything inside) but scientists suggest staying at least 30 or 40 metres away as evening approaches so as not to disturb them.

How many of these different field signs will you discover? (They may not all be possible, depending on where you are and the time of day.)

(1) Tracks. Kiwi tracks show three toes similar to other birds. This is the same as dinosaurs, which birds are closely related to. I learnt to identify kiwi tracks from their thicker toes and larger size compared to other birds.

(2) Poo. Kiwi poo is not always this large. Like most other birds the poo and wee are done at the same time creating a combination of black poo and white wee. A large blob of bird poo like this is likely to be a kiwi.

(3) Poke holes. Kiwis will use their long bills to poke into the ground. They then often move their bill around making the hole larger like in this photograph. Sometimes you can see an area of ground with lots of holes like this.

(4) Burrow. This is a Little Spotted Kiwi burrow I saw on Kapiti Island.

(5) Listen! Are you a light sleeper? Are you staying in or near a kiwi hotspot? Listen out at night for their distinctive call.

Australasia Seawatching (Activity)

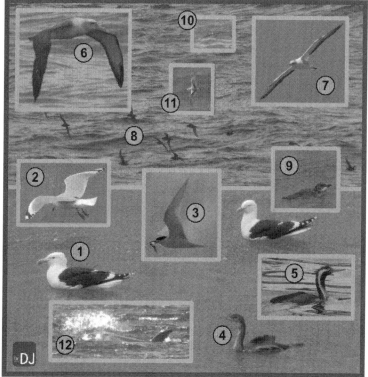

Here are different animals and behaviours to look for along the coast of Australasia. (They may not all be possible, depending on where you are and the time of year.)

(1) Large gulls. Larger gulls such as Kelp Gull (also known as Black-backed Gull) are found by the coast. Along with other animals they will follow fishing boats looking for fish parts that are thrown overboard.

(2) Small gulls. Smaller gulls such as Red-billed Gull (also known as Silver Gull) live inland and on the coast.

(3) Fishing. Can you see an animal catching a fish? This White-fronted Tern is carrying a fish, probably back to its nest (as research into terns has shown this is a common thing so as to carry food back to the young).

(4) Swimming under the water. Cormorants/shags sit on the water and dive to swim underwater hunting fish.

(5) Patterns. Some cormorants/shags such as this Spotted Shag have different-coloured feathers that create patterns in their plumage.

(6) Albatross. Australasia is a great place to see albatross. Many species are only found here and they are fairly common, even coming close to shore in some places.

(7) Powerful divers. Australasian Gannet are powerful flyers that dive hard into the water when they see a fish.

(8) Flocks over the water. I have seen groups of shearwater out at sea from ferries. These Short-tailed Shearwater are particularly common offshore of Tasmania.

(9) Penguins. Compared to other birds, penguins float low in the water. I mainly see penguins on the beach at dawn and dusk. If I see one I keep my distance so as not to stress them.

(10) Specialist seabirds. Storm-petrels are generally difficult to spot because they are so small. I have always seen them after carefully scanning the water with my binoculars.

(11) Prions. I have mainly seen prions out at sea. I have regularly seen Fairy Prion around New Zealand and Tasmania.

(12) Dolphins. It can be difficult to see dolphins. I often find them by looking carefully at the water where birds are circling: birds and dolphins are both carnivorous so can collect together around a large shoal of fish.

This book is part of the Nature Travel Guide series.

Other books in the series cover different countries and one covers general wildlife watching skills.

Love nature, be loved in return.

If you "follow" me on Amazon you can get updates about new books that I write. Here are three example links to my author homepage on Amazon: (UK, US and Germany)

https://www.amazon.co.uk/Duncan-James/e/B00U0O1NOI

https://www.amazon.com/author/drduncanjames

https://www.amazon.de/Duncan-James/e/B00U0O1NOI

If you enjoy this book it would be great if you could rate and/or review to help others to find it.

However, if this book doesn't work for you then perhaps tell me so that I can try to fix it both for you and for other readers.

My email is drduncanjames@gmail.com and I welcome your feedback, your questions or simply your friendly correspondence.

I have a YouTube channel with content to complement many of my books:

https://www.youtube.com/drduncanjames

Printed in Great Britain
by Amazon